By the same author

A GUIDE TO DRIVING HORSES (Pelham Books)
LOOKING AT CARRIAGES (Pelham Books)
BREAKING A HORSE TO HARNESS (J. A. Allen)
FUNDAMENTALS OF PRIVATE DRIVING
(British Driving Society)
THE ENCYCLOPAEDIA OF CARRIAGE DRIVING
(J. A. Allen)

Handling Your Problem Horse

Sallie Walrond

SWAN·HILL
PRESS

First published in the UK in 1982 by Pelham Books
Published 1993 as *Your Problem Horse* by Swan Hill Press
an imprint of Airlife Publishing Ltd
This edition 1998

British Library Cataloguing-in-Publication Data
  A catalogue record for this book
  is available from the British Library

ISBN 1 84037 088 2

The information in this book is true and complete to the best of our knowledge. All recommendations are made without any guarantee on the part of the publisher, who also disclaims any liability incurred in connection with the use of this data or specific details.

Printed in England by St Edmundsbury Press Ltd, Bury St Edmunds, Suffolk.

Swan Hill Press

an imprint of Airlife Publishing Ltd
101 Longden Road, Shrewsbury, SY3 9EB, England

DEDICATION

This book is dedicated to my mother and to my late father who made it possible for me to pursue a career with horses, and to Dickie and the late Robert Barley who taught me to ride, drive and handle all kinds of horses.

CONTENTS

ACKNOWLEDGEMENTS

The author thanks Anne Grahame Johnstone for taking such care and trouble with the line drawings.

She is grateful to Mrs Derek Hatley for transforming pages of nearly indecipherable long-hand into immaculate typescript.

She also thanks Mr and Mrs Sanders Watney for their help with the text.

INTRODUCTION

Increasing numbers of people are discovering the pleasures, as well as the difficulties, which can be derived from keeping horses and ponies for riding and driving.

Gone are the days when most large households employed an experienced groom who would produce well-mannered horses for the family, both as a means of transport and for pleasure purposes. People, in general, had some knowledge of horses. Grooms were probably trained by their fathers. Bad habits in horses were automatically dealt with by these true horsemen. Horses were plentiful so it is likely that really difficult ones were discarded from private service. They were probably sold to horse dealers who sorted them out and passed them back into private service again. Extreme cases were perhaps put to work in a night coach. If all else failed, they quite likely ended up at the knacker.

Now, in the late twentieth century, many of the people who keep horses and ponies have not been brought up with a 'horsy' background. They have little or no knowledge of the way in which a horse thinks. They bravely embark on purchasing a horse or pony and then encounter numerous problems which appear to be insurmountable. The newcomer is frequently afraid of spoiling the animal by dealing with the difficulty in the wrong way and so the problem worsens and becomes thoroughly established.

This book is not directed at experienced horsemen who will have worked out their own ways of dealing with the problems mentioned in these pages.

The methods which are suggested are those which the author has found to be effective over her years of teaching pupils and training horses to ride and drive.

Most problems with horses are initially created by

man. Very few foals are born with wicked thoughts in their heads. Difficulties are often created by bad management which has caused fear on the part of the horse.

Horses have incredibly good memories and if they receive a fright they will probably never forget it. They are usually not blessed with great intelligence but by patient handling, and repetition of commands, they can be taught to do all kinds of things.

Once a horse has fully understood what is required he will usually work willingly and tirelessly for his owner and give his best whenever it is required. A bond can be built between the human and the horse which gives years of pleasure to them both.

Unfortunately, when a horse changes hands to a new owner, the vendor does not always admit the difficulties he has encountered, and problems occur which can cause distress for all concerned. If only the horse could talk, so that he could explain his fear, then life would be considerably easier for both the handler and his horse.

When a problem is encountered it is best to consider, first of all, what the cause might be. Then, thoughts should turn to preventing the problem from recurring. Finally, if the problem persists, it must be dealt with so that the handler can cope with the animal and master the situation.

It is hoped that the ideas put forward will be of some help to newcomers to horse ownership and prevent some of the heartache which horses can cause.

THE SMELL OF FEAR

It is a well-known and accepted fact that fear felt by a rider, driver or associate, in any given situation, is quickly sensed by the horse which is being handled.

Nearly all problems with horses are caused, initially, by fear of some kind. It is therefore essential that any fear which is felt by a handler, should not be transmitted to the horse.

If a person is afraid, then adrenalin rushes through his body in order to put it into top gear so that he is able to deal with the anticipated difficulty. The handler does not have to be actually afraid for this to happen. In fact, mere knowledge that a situation may cause trouble is enough to cause adrenalin to flow readily. The smell is immediately noticed by the horse who receives the signal as a warning that something frightening is about to happen. He is alerted for impending danger and instantly becomes tense. This reaction naturally makes his handler more nervous. The situation has completed a full circle and can only get worse. The end product is a nervous trainer and equally nervous horse who will not be in a position to give much moral support to each other.

Obviously, this is of no help in coping with difficulties. When problems have to be overcome it is essential that the handler should appear unafraid even if, in fact, he is feeling rather apprehensive about the whole thing.

The answer is provided by the use of the equine aromatic called 'Pax', which can be obtained from Day, Son and Hewitt of St. George's Quay, Lancaster LA1 5QJ. A little is rubbed onto the hands and forehead before any difficult or frightening occasion has to be faced. Any smell of adrenalin which is given off, is masked by the aroma of Pax. The horse is fascinated by the scent, does not smell the adrenalin and so remains calm. In turn, the trainer becomes less afraid because he knows that the horse cannot smell that he is apprehensive. The whole situation remains far calmer than if Pax were not used.

Horse oils were used by the men who travelled with stallions at the beginning of the century. All kinds of mysterious theories are put forward referring to calming potions to help with the handling of fierce horses. So the idea is neither new nor magical.

It seems sensible to make use of any available help when difficult horses have to be handled and one as simple as an aromatic cannot be ignored.

CORRECTION

It is overwhelmingly important not to punish a horse at the wrong time.

Conversely, it is important to correct a horse immediately he has done something which is deliberately disobedient. Tremendous and lasting damage can be done to a horse who does not understand why he is being hit. The trainer must make an instant decision as to whether the horse was being difficult because he was afraid or whether he was just being naughty. If the horse is punished for being afraid he will become worse. If he is being naughty then he must be corrected instantly. It is no earthly good hitting him minutes after he has committed the crime. He must be corrected the very moment that he is disobedient.

A horse must never be hit when the trainer is in a temper. A horse can be ruined for life if he is given a hiding by someone who is almost blind with fury. The horse may never fully recover. The author knows of one horse who was turned from a gentle and kind hack into a vicious kicking and biting brute, in a matter of months, by what she suspects was an unwarranted beating by a drunken owner. The horse, who had trusted people, became so vicious that he hated all humanity, which was very sad.

Obviously, a horse must be corrected firmly for outright naughtiness. One strong vocal remonstration is enough for some horses. This is preferable to constant nagging which the horse soon gets used to and eventually ceases to notice.

A difficult horse is usually an unhappy horse.

THE PROBLEMS

Difficult to Catch

A horse or pony who is difficult to catch can be infuriating. Many hours will be wasted walking after an animal who skilfully manages to keep just out of reach of the person who is trying to catch him. If cornered, such an animal will either submit to defeat or make a dash for freedom and may knock over anyone who happens to be in his way.

Cause

The habit is probably caused by the horse relating being caught to something unpleasant.

It is a great mistake to go out into the field with a bridle, put it onto the unsuspecting horse then lead him to the gate to be saddled and ridden without any reward for his co-operation. He will quite likely walk away the next time he is approached by someone carrying a bridle or headcollar. If he does walk away and is then caught after a few minutes it is a grave error to punish him for his misdemeanour. He will not understand why he is in trouble and will be worse next time.

Prevention

The horse should associate being caught with getting fed and having a fuss made of him.

It is best to leave a headcollar on the horse in the early stages of training. He should be caught and led into his stable for a feed, which he must be left to enjoy and digest in peace before he is worked.

In order to train a difficult and shy horse it is best to go to the field several times a day with a small amount of particularly appetizing food in a bucket. The field should be small and not have much grass. The horse should be called by name and the food transferred to a feed bin. The principle of this method is to persuade the horse to come to his trainer as opposed to his trainer having to go to him. If the horse is very nervous, it is probably best to turn and walk away. Gradually, the horse will learn to look forward to the visits and will eventually come up to the bin whilst his trainer is standing beside it. It is wisest to make no attempt to put a hand onto the headcollar until the horse has become entirely confident. If he jumps away, a lot of harm may be done. As time progresses, the horse will probably allow his trainer to put a hand onto his neck and then his head. Eventually, he can be caught. It is sometimes a help to have a piece of rope, about 6 inches (15 cms) long, fixed to the rear ring of the headcollar. This is easier to hold. He should then be caressed and once the atmosphere is fully happy and relaxed he can be allowed to go free. When he discovers that the trainer is associated with food and being stroked he will almost certainly submit to being caught quite easily. It is essential to make at least two daily visits for this purpose in order to build up confidence in the horse.

Dealing with the problem

There are various methods of dealing immediately with horses who are difficult to catch if it is essential that they are turned out in a field.

Horses of thoroughbred or Arab blood probably will not tolerate these methods but they have been proved to be effective with ponies and cobs of mountain and moorland breeding.

A tethering peg can be hammered into the ground and a heavy chain which is about 15 feet (4.5 metres) long, with links of about 1½ inches (35 mm), is fastened with a shackle and swivel to the peg. The chain is attached by means of a shackle, swivel, shackle and spring hook (see Fig. 1) to a wide neckstrap which is buckled around the horse's neck. The swivels are important because they prevent the chain from becoming twisted. The horse soon learns that he cannot escape and stands quietly to be caught.

With this method there is a danger of the chain getting caught round a hind heel which could cause injury. It is for this reason that rope, or a lungeing rein, must *never* be used for tethering. A serious rope burn, resulting in permanent injury, is very likely to be caused by these. Heavy chain will drop away from the heel. Light chain is unsuitable as it could cut into the pastern and sever a tendon.

Some gypsies train their young horses to tether by fixing a substantial weight, which the horse is *just* able to move, onto the end of the chain. Then, when he gets a leg caught in the chain, the weight moves when he pulls to free himself. He soon learns how to disentangle his leg when it becomes caught on the chain and will quietly step back to loosen the chain the required amount for it to fall to the ground. Horses which are used to being tethered become expert at untangling themselves and rarely get into a muddle.

Another option is to leave the end of the chain un-

Fig. 1 Shackle, swivel, shackle
and spring hook for attaching
chain to neckstrap.

fastened. There is a danger of the horse galloping with
the chain flying out behind and apparently chasing him.
However, once he has become used to the chain it will
be found that he can be caught by getting hold of the
end which is some distance from the horse's head. If this
method is used, the chain must be fastened to the headcollar, otherwise the horse will quickly learn that, in a
neckstrap he can pull away from the person trying to
catch him. Care must be taken not to get a finger caught

in the links of the chain, which could result in serious injury to, or even loss of, a finger.

It is not really safe to leave a horse unattended on a chain in case he gets caught up. The method is only meant for giving a horse a short period of grass daily and for teaching him to be caught.

Another method is to put hobbles onto the horse. These resemble two wide dog collars which are padded with thick felt. They are strapped round the front pasterns and joined together by their dees with two large shackles (see Fig. 2). Some were designed with quick-release systems but it is more usual to have buckles. The horse can walk with short steps to graze but is prevented from trotting. It is possible, however, for a determined pony to proceed at a pace which resembles a canter with both front feet going forward together. Hobbles usually act as a deterrent to ponies who are slightly difficult to catch, providing they are approached carefully with the training method which is earlier described.

Chains and hobbles *must not* be used on nervous horses as they will almost certainly injure themselves.

Fig. 2 Hobbles.

A method which is effective and safer than chains and hobbles is to construct a large pen with high fences into which the horse can be lured either by food or another horse. The rails are then put up behind him once he is safely inside the pen and he can then probably be caught.

Another method, which sometimes works, involves as many people as are available (at least five) and a long piece of rope. The rope is carried at about 3 feet (1 metre) from the ground (unless the pony is of Shetland size) and held in a straight line by everyone. The horse is gradually cornered and then approached by just one person whilst everyone else holds the barrier rope. Great care should be taken to hold the rope in such a way that if the horse should charge at it to escape, it (the rope) is free to go loose without anyone getting knocked over. The rope must be held behind all the 'catchers' so that when the horse is cornered, the people are nearer to the horse than is the rope. If the horse then gallops into the rope, the holders can let go and it will fly out of their hands without knocking them off their feet. It is not possible to hold a horse if he makes a dash for freedom. The only hope, with this method, is that the horse will think that the barrier is impenetrable and will allow himself to be caught. Once he has discovered that he has only to charge at the rope for freedom, the method will not be effective.

There are some horses who can be caught by a method which involves persistent walking by the person who is trying to catch them. The technique is to follow the horse quietly wherever he goes until eventually he allows himself to be caught. This can take a considerable time. It is useless, and in fact harmful, to run if he gallops away. He will enjoy the game and gallop even faster.

A horse which is awkward to catch will be easier if he is turned out alone. It is very difficult to catch a horse when he has a friend to accompany him as he gallops off. Also, the friend will probably get in the way as he tries to eat the enticing food and will even chase the nervous one and make matters worse.

If, for some reason, the horse has been turned out without a headcollar, great care must be taken when approaching him, to keep the halter or headcollar which is to be used to catch him, concealed from his view. The oat scoop or bucket should be held in one hand whilst the headcollar is held in the other hand behind the back. Then the trainer should try to stand alongside the horse's shoulder and as he eats, the head-collar can be slipped around the horse's neck. It is a great mistake to approach the horse head-on with the headcollar in an outstretched hand. He will almost certainly turn away. Most quiet horses will give in once the headcollar has been passed around their neck from behind.

Difficult to Lead

Horses who pull either forwards or backwards when they are being led are a nuisance.

Cause

This resistance is usually due to failure on the part of the breeder to train the animal to lead as a foal.

Prevention

Foals should be halter broken when they are only a few days old. A foal-sized leather headcollar should be put on. This is preferable to a foal-slip which is inclined to rub against the foal's eyes and make him sore. A long leading rein or lunge rein should be fixed to the back ring of the headcollar. This enables the foal to be played without risk of letting go or pulling him over backwards if he should try to rush away from his handler. It is a help to have an assistant who can put his arms around the foal's hindquarters to propel him forward if he is reluctant to walk on. This is preferable to pulling on his head which will probably teach him to resist. Also, he may get hurt if he is pulled along. The foal will soon learn to go for walks alongside or behind his mother and will accept being led. It is very important that he is led from alternate sides on alternate lessons so that he does not become one-sided. Youngsters who are never led from the off-side will be difficult to lunge to the right and will probably favour working to the left at all paces throughout their lives.

Dealing with the problem

Mature horses who are known to pull forwards or sideways to escape should not be led in a headcollar. It is very often easier to hold such a horse with a breaking cavesson. A lunge rein should be fixed to the central ring on the front of the nose-piece. The horse's face can then be turned towards the handler if the animal should try to use his head, neck and shoulder to pull away.

If the horse is strong and inclined to pull forward it may be preferable to use a bridle. If a bridle has to be used then it is best to pass the lunge rein through the near-side ring of the bit and over the head before buckling it to the off-side ring. This results in a gag-type action if the horse should try to pull away. It is very strong and will be found to give greater control than if the rein is passed through the bit rings and behind the jaw before it is buckled to the outer bit ring. This latter method tends to turn the horse's head away from the handler which puts the horse at an advantage. If the rein is buckled only to the ring which is nearest to the handler there is a danger of the bit being pulled through the horse's mouth if he should try to get away.

If the horse hangs back then the trainer should enlist the aid of another person to walk behind the horse and persuade him forward with a lungeing whip. He can then be patted by his leader for coming alongside. He should be trained to walk so that his shoulder is level with that of his handler.

If the trainer is alone it is a help to hold a long whip in the left hand whilst the horse is being led from the near-side with the right hand. The whip can then be used on the horse's quarters to encourage him forward if he should try to hang back. When he comes alongside he should be caressed so he knows he is doing what is required.

Reluctance to being Tied Up

Horses which cannot be tied up are a bore. Broken head-collars, pulled down fences and loose horses are usually the result of such reluctance.

A horse must *never* be tied up by the reins of his bridle. One quick jerk will tear the head-piece or break the reins.

Cause

This habit is generally caused by the horse initially discovering that if he pulls backwards hard enough, something usually gives way to his enormous strength. Once he has discovered this he will apply these tactics whenever he decides that he does not want to remain tied up.

Prevention

The secret of training a horse to be tied up is to never let him break free. His education should be started when he is young. He should be tied to a solid post, tree, or ring in a wall which will not give way however much he pulls backwards. It is better to use a rope halter, with a throatlash so that it cannot slip off, than a leather head-collar for this training. Leather headcollars are inclined to break if they are subjected to sudden and heavy jerks. For this reason, brass hooks and unsound ropes are not suitable for training as they also tend to give way under stress.

Dealing with the problem

If the horse is known to be difficult to tie up, then it is safer not to attempt to leave him tied in a situation such as a showground where, if he got free, disaster may occur. Horses have such good memories that they will never forget how easily they have managed to free themselves in the past. Some horses can never be completely trustworthy about being tied up. However, if the animal in question is still young, and at a stage where he is merely experimenting with the idea of pulling back, it may be possible to train him to remain secured to a ring or similar fixture. An effective method of training is to put a lunge rein onto the headcollar. This is then passed through a ring on the wall and the end is held by the trainer who can play it out if the horse tries to go backwards. It can then be pulled back through the ring to bring the horse forward again. He will discover that his pulling back did not free him. This training operation can be combined with a grooming session and will be found to be effective. When the horse is later tied in the stable for reasons such as mucking out then care must be taken to use a halter or very strong headcollar which will not break.

It is best not to use a rack chain for a doubtful horse because, should he pull back against the chain, the shock to the headcollar and the ring in the wall will be much greater.

Bad to Box

A horse who will not load can be very tiresome. It is usually disastrous if this happens at the start of the day when a long journey lies ahead. Tempers quickly become frayed and the horse gets more upset. Equally, an animal which staunchly refuses to go into his trailer on a crowded showground at the end of the day, can be particularly embarrassing. It is usually only a matter of minutes before numerous, well-meaning helpers will appear with conflicting advice.

Cause

Horses can become hard to box for several reasons. Careless driving could cause this problem. When transporting horses, it is essential to drive smoothly. Sudden or violent applications of the brakes or accelerator, or fast cornering, can throw a horse off his feet. If this happens he will naturally become frightened of travelling. He will then be unwilling to load because he will know he is likely to have an unpleasant time in the trailer.

Horses usually prefer to have a padded partition on which to lean sideways. A breast bar is also an advantage. The horse's chest will then go against this and his head will be protected from hitting the front of the trailer if the driver is forced suddenly to brake.

The warmth of the horse should be considered and

sheets or rugs must be put on as necessary to keep the horse comfortable. However, there is the danger of putting on too many rugs and the horse becoming too hot.

Some horses are frightened by the sight of heavy lorries following close behind. At night, headlights flashing into the trailer can also cause fear. It is then a good idea to close the rear top doors.

Prevention

If the horse has been correctly trained to load, and never gets a fright when travelling, he will probably always walk quietly into a horsebox or trailer.

He must, in the early stages, be made to regard his trailer as a stable. It should be welcoming in that it is comfortable and contains food. He will then not object to being boxed.

The training method is simple although it may take several weeks to complete if the horse has a nervous temperament. A four-wheeled, front unload, double trailer is best for teaching a horse to load.

It is advisable to remove the partition to begin with so that the entrance looks wide and inviting. If the horse hits his hip on the first introduction to boxing, it is likely that his owner will have trouble the next time he tries to persuade the animal to load.

The trailer should be carefully positioned with the rear ramp alongside a wall which will act as a 'wing'. If the trailer can be reversed into a passageway of some kind, so much the better. Another useful gambit is to back the trailer up to a double garage or similar construction (but not the horse's own stable). The horse is led in through the next-door building and the doors are shut behind him. The trailer offers the only way out.

The front jockey wheel should be let down and firmly secured. The rear jacks should also be put down and fastened. The brake must be put on. This all ensures

that the trailer will stand firmly. On no account should
it rock or move when the horse walks up the ramp. It
is important, too, to make sure that the ramp is steady
when it is on the ground. A block of wood or a brick is
often needed at one side to hold it level.

Having carefully set the stage, the time comes to load
the horse. Under no circumstances should this be
attempted if the trainer is in a hurry. It is a good plan
to feed all the horses other than the one which is to be
loaded. Breakfast time is best. He will probably be
hungrier then than later in the day. After about ten
minutes, when he is beginning to get really worried about
his food, a lungeing cavesson can be put on. The lower
noseband strap should be left looser than usual so that
he can open his mouth to eat. A lungeing rein is buckled
to the centre dee on the noseband. This gives greater
control than would be obtained from a headcollar and
rope if the horse should be difficult on this first attempt.
The trainer should take the bucket of food and walk
towards the trailer with the horse. If the animal is young,
innocent and has a pony temperament it is possible that
he will walk gingerly up the ramp after his breakfast. If
he has a nervous temperament he will probably stop at
the bottom of the ramp. He must not be tugged by his
head. A horse cannot be pulled anywhere. He must be
caressed and tempted. He should not be hit. He should
be persuaded with the command 'Walk on' or whatever
he understands from his work on the lunge or in hand.
The food is held tantalizingly just out of reach. It is
often a help to place one front foot on the ramp. He
may be reluctant to put his weight on that foot but if
his handler, or an assistant, then lifts the other front leg
and places the hoof onto the ramp he will be forced to
stand on it and will gain confidence. The problem is
usually caused, at this stage, by the horse not trusting
the ramp to take his weight. Patience is essential.

With some horses, the trainer should be satisfied that
he has got as far as this on the first day and the horse

should be allowed to eat his breakfast whilst standing with two front feet on the ramp. This should be repeated daily and gradually the horse will walk into the trailer after his breakfast. The ramp must not be put up until the horse has the whole of both of his hind feet inside the trailer. If he feels that one hind leg is being lifted by the ramp he is almost certain to rush backwards and a lot of harm will have been done, not to say, injury to the handlers. A fright which is caused by this impatience could take several days to put right.

When the ramp has been put up the horse must be allowed to finish his feed. He can either be tied up and left, if some means of hooking the manger can be devised, or he can be held by his trainer. He should not be left loose because he will probably try to turn round. He may fall over. He could try to jump out over the back ramp. Care must be taken if the partition is out, and therefore there are no breast bars, that the little door at the side is firmly shut. It is possible for a pony to get halfway out of this narrow door and become jammed with the door post between his hips and his ribs.

When he has finished his feed, the front ramp can be let down and the horse allowed to walk out. Usually, if this routine is carried out daily for about a week, without a hitch, he will begin to look forward to being loaded. He will enjoy the attention. He will be prepared to walk through the trailer as easily as he goes in and out of his stable. A small reward, such as a peppermint, will suffice. The advantage of a front unload trailer is that the horse never learns to back out. Once he discovers how easy it is to step backwards he may use this as a resistance.

If the only trailer available is one without a front ramp for unloading, then care must be taken to train the horse not to rush out backwards as soon as the rear ramp is let down. For training purposes it is best to open the middle partition, at the rear, and leave the front secured. As soon as the horse has walked into the trailer, an assistant should put up the ramp. Then, the partition can be put across from the inside and secured. The breeching chain can be hooked across behind the horse. For this purpose a chain enclosed in hosepipe is preferable to webbing, which is inclined to break if the horse sits against it when the ramp is let down.

When the horse has finished his feed, he must be untied and then the rear ramp can be let down. The breeching chain should prevent the horse from stepping out. He must be made to stand forward whilst the chain is unhooked by the assistant. The horse can then be told to back out by the trainer, who has been at his head throughout this manoeuvre. He should be encouraged to walk out quietly, one step at a time. It will be a help to have a lunge rein in preference to a rope so that if he tries to rush out backwards, the handler is not afraid of being compelled to let go. This added confidence may help the situation.

It will be found, eventually, that the horse can be boxed single-handed. The feed manger can be hooked over the breast bar beforehand, and the horse will walk into the trailer on his own to get his breakfast. The handler can clip the breeching chain across and put up the rear ramp. He can then go through the groom's door, at the front, and tie the headcollar rope to the ring so that the horse will not try to turn and get into a muddle.

Even if the horse has been trained to load in the above way, it is advisable to box him a few days before an important journey is planned as a reminder. This small precaution can prevent a drama on the occasion, when perhaps everyone is a little on edge and adrenalin is flowing.

Dealing with the problem

Two lungeing reins and a nylon lungeing whip should be kept in the horsebox so that they are always available if the problem should arise.

If difficulty in loading is experienced, it is best to open the rear end of the dividing partition if the horse is being boxed into a double trailer. He is much more likely to load if the entrance is widened.

The lunge reins should be buckled onto the rings or pins on the sides at the rear of the trailer. Two people take the ends of the lunge reins and a third person leads the horse towards the ramp. A fourth person encourages the reluctant animal forward with the lungeing whip. As the horse goes between the lunge reins they are crossed behind him, around his quarters, as the handlers change sides. It is usually advantageous to flick the whip towards the horse at this stage. The combination of the crossing reins and whip usually results in the horse going into the trailer. It is, however, essential to carry out the operation with planning and a sense of purpose so that the horse is loaded before he realizes that it is happening.

The ramp must be put up very quickly and the pins fastened before the horse flies out backwards. For this reason, it is essential to stand to the sides of the ramp when it is put up. Half a ton of horse retreating backwards at speed can force the ramp down on top of whoever is unfortunate enough to be standing below it. The result could be fatal.

If the horse is known to be a doubtful loader it is better to 'set the stage' with the lunge reins, than to have to resort to this method after he has begun to resist. He will probably be more difficult to load once he has already said 'No'.

Often, the system mentioned above, of backing the trailer into the entrance of a building which is strange to the horse, can be very successful indeed, even with an established bad loader.

One harness horse who had suddenly become difficult to box, was apparently persuaded to load by being long-reined into the horsebox. His driving bridle was put on and he was driven from behind with no problem. Of course, if this system is used with a trailer, it is essential to put the central partition to one side because the blinkers will prevent the horse from seeing sideways. He may hit his ribs or knock his hips as he walks into the trailer, and this would probably create more difficulties.

Difficult to Bridle or Unbridle

Difficulties in putting on and taking off a bridle are fairly common. These problems are of particular nuisance to a child or small adult if the animal is tall. The horse quickly realizes that he only has to raise his head to evade his handler.

Cause

The problem is generally caused by bad breaking or care- less handling. The horse has probably had the bit banged against his incisors when his handler failed to open the animal's mouth when putting the bridle on. Alternatively, he may have had his ears roughly pulled between the head-piece and browband. The maltreatment may have occurred when the horse was being unbridled. A careless handler perhaps failed to unbuckle the noseband so the horse was not able to open his mouth sufficiently to release the bit. The curb chain may not have been un- hooked so the curb bit caught against the lower incisors as the chain was held by the chin. This would make the horse throw his head upwards. If the handler snatched the bridle away, the horse would receive a blow from the bit against the teeth. Quite rightly, he will object to such treatment and will almost certainly become difficult to bridle and/or unbridle.

Prevention

It is essential to take extreme care when putting on or removing a bridle so that the operation does not cause any discomfort to the horse.

When bridling the horse, the head-piece should be held in the right hand as the handler stands alongside the near-side of the horse's neck. The left hand is placed below the bit. If a double bridle is being put on, then the bridoon should be placed over the Weymouth so that the bits will go into the horse's mouth as one. The central finger of the left hand should be put gently into the off-side of the horse's mouth at the corner. There are no teeth here, so it is quite safe. The horse, on feeling the finger going into the corner of his mouth, will part his incisors to take the bit. The left thumb should be placed under the bit to guide it upwards as soon as he opens his mouth. Another satisfactory method is to insert the thumb of the left hand into the near-side of the mouth and to use the fingers of the left hand to guide the bit. Anyhow, once the horse opens his mouth, the head-piece can be raised with the right hand while the left hand carefully brings the ears into place. The mane and forelock must then be divided and the horse made comfortable.

If the bridle is always put on in this manner, the horse will not be distressed and there should never be a problem.

The noseband, throatlash and curb chain are fastened once the bridle is in place. Before the bridle is removed it is essential that these should be unfastened.

The head-piece must be taken gently over the horse's ears and lowered. The bit must never be dragged from the horse's mouth if he has not opened his incisors. It is important to wait until he has parted his teeth before the bridle is taken from his face.

Dealing with the problem

If the horse is very difficult to bridle then it is a help to unbuckle the reins and remove the cheek-pieces on both sides. The head-piece and browband are put over the poll and ears. The off-side cheek-piece can now be buckled to the head-piece. The bit is easier to get into the mouth from one side than from under the incisors. The near-side cheek-piece can now be buckled to the head-piece. Finally the reins are attached to the bit. It is probably best to leave the noseband off for the first few days as its addition may make the operation more difficult.

Some horses appreciate their bit warmed before it is put into their mouths. Others become better to bridle if syrup or honey is put onto the bit. There is the dis-advantage of the stickiness in handling such an object but it is worth the mess if the horse becomes easier to bridle as a result.

It is best to seek veterinary advice if the horse persists in being difficult. He may have tooth problems, or ear trouble.

Difficult to Saddle

A few horses can be bad to saddle. They object to the girth being tightened and hump their backs or blow themselves out. Very often, such an animal will stand with his front legs slightly apart when he is saddled. Then, as he is led forward, he will leap into the air and plunge. Such behaviour is unpleasant, inconvenient and dangerous.

Cause

This problem was probably caused, initially, by careless breaking. If, when the horse was first introduced to wearing a roller, he was girthed too tightly, too soon, he may have developed the habits of both humping his back and blowing himself out. Careless saddling of a carefully broken horse can make him nervous of having his skin pinched between the end of the saddle flap and the girth. Inevitably, he will blow himself out to ease the situation. Sometimes, a hunter will become sore from friction caused by the tops of hunting boots at the bottom of the saddle flap. This can make him wary of being hurt when he is girthed. Girth galls can also cause an animal to cringe at the thought of being saddled. These mostly occur with unfit horses when sweat builds up around the girth area under the horse's arms. If the horse is not kept clean and if the girth is not regularly washed or saddle-soaped, depending on whether it is of nylon or of leather, the animal can soon become very sore, swollen, or even develop an open wound. Once this happens, he will understandably be reluctant to be saddled. He may react by either humping his back or by biting the person who is saddling him.

Horses who are cold-backed — that is, those who dislike the coldness of a saddle on their backs — can also be a problem.

Prevention

When a saddle is put on, it must be laid gently above the withers, with the girth placed over the seat, and carefully slid back, with the direction of the coat, until it lies in position behind the withers. The girth can then be put down gently, passed under the girth of the horse and buckled loosely onto the point straps. Once the horse has relaxed, the girth can be taken up, one hole at a time, until it is buckled barely tightly enough to hold the saddle in position. The horse is then led out to be mounted and the girth can be tightened again before mounting. Once the rider has mounted, the girth can be tightened yet again.

It is essential to see that the girth is always scrupulously clean and that the lining of the saddle is always free from grease or dirt of any kind when it is put on.

If the horse is cold-backed then it is best to use a sheepskin or similar numnah, so that he does not have to put up with a cold leather lining on his back. It is also a good idea to saddle such an animal at least a quarter of an hour before he is ridden so that his back has time to warm the numnah. Such precautions will help to prevent him from bucking when he is mounted.

Dealing with the problem

Obviously, the saddle and girth must be clean, soft and comfortable. A numnah should be used. If the horse dislikes the feeling of a girth, he should be made to live in a roller for twenty-four hours a day, in the stable, so that he gradually learns to accept the pressure around his body.

Great care must be taken when saddling to ensure that the horse is never girthed tightly, too quickly. He must be treated with kindness and care. It is safest not to tie him up when he is being saddled, but to run a long rope or lunge rein through a ring on the wall so that if he should fly backwards he can be played out and then gently brought forward again. If he is fixed to the wall whilst he is plunging from being girthed, he may throw himself onto the floor.

Any signs of girth soreness must be dealt with immediately by applying a skin hardener. It is often best to get a solution from a veterinary surgeon, as this is more likely to be effective than the usual salt and water or methylated spirit hardeners which are so often used. These, in any case, must never be applied to broken skin.

Difficult to Mount

Quite a lot of horses are disobedient about standing still when they are mounted. The habit can create great difficulty for a small rider if the horse is large and the occasion exciting. The rider, who is likely to be wearing tight breeches, hops on his right foot whilst the horse goes round in circles taking the rider's left foot with him, in the stirrup.

Cause

Some horses are never taught to stand to be mounted when they are broken in so the fault lies with the trainer. Others which have been good to mount can be made difficult by a careless rider.

Some people are very rough when they climb onto a horse's back. They begin by picking up one rein much tighter than the other so that the horse is forced to stand with his head held to one side, making him feel unbalanced. The rider then places his foot into the stirrup and perhaps digs his toe into the animal's ribs. He then hauls himself towards the horse, by the saddle, causing it to be pulled sideways off the centre of the horse's spine. The girth is wrenched around the belly. Next, he perhaps hits the unfortunate horse on the quarters with his right foot, before finally landing into the saddle with a thump.

It is no wonder that an animal who is treated in this way will soon become anxious about being mounted and will be inclined to walk away.

Some horses simply become difficult to mount because their rider does not insist that they stand. They become more and more disobedient until they walk away purely by habit.

Failing to tighten the girth adequately before mounting, so that the saddle rotates when weight is put onto the stirrup, can frighten a newly broken youngster and cause problems.

Prevention

It is essential, during early training, to mount from a block of some kind so that the horse always stands still. He should be rewarded before being asked to move off. He will then, if he is treated correctly, remain motionless to be mounted throughout his life.

Dealing with the problem

The rider must be prepared to spend time in training the horse to stand. The horse should be positioned, ready to be mounted, in a corner so that he is prevented from stepping sideways, away from his rider, by one barrier and from moving forwards by another. If he is inclined to resist by going backwards, he must be placed in such a way that he reverses into a wall or similar obstruction if he steps back. Wire fences must not be used as barriers. A portable mounting block, such as a straw bale or caravan step, is then placed alongside the near-side of the horse, level with the stirrup. This will enable the rider to reach the stirrup easily and mount without putting any sideways strain onto the saddle. It also enables the rider not to dig his toe into the horse's ribs.

The rider should climb onto the mounting block and prepare carefully to mount. The horse must be made to stand absolutely still and be re-positioned repeatedly if he tries to walk away. The reins must be picked up so that a level contact is taken on the horse's mouth to keep him still. They are then held in the left hand. It is a help, if there are difficulties, to have an assistant who can give the horse a titbit to make him look forward to being mounted.

When the left foot is placed in the stirrup it is essential to point the toe downwards so that it does not dig into the horse's ribs. As the rider mounts he should press his right hand down on the right side of the front of the saddle to balance the weight which is being taken by the left stirrup. The right leg must be carefully swung over the horse's quarters. The rider should then lower himself gently into the seat of the saddle.

The horse can now be rewarded with a titbit either by the assistant or, if no help is available, by the rider. Later, the titbit can be given by the rider as a matter of course. The horse will learn to stand quite still, in anticipation of his reward. He will soon think that it is pleasant to be mounted. He can be moved away from the barriers, one at a time, and mounted from any available ledge. Finally he will be prepared to stand to be mounted from the ground.

Overbending

Horses which overbend (carry their heads with their necks bent at the crest with their faces behind the perpendicular) can be very hard to control. When their rider or driver puts pressure onto the horse's mouth with the reins, in order to slow down or stop, the horse resists by lowering his head, dropping the bit and bringing his chin towards his chest. The rider or driver is then left to pull against the horse's neck and so is at a great disadvantage.

Cause

Horses frequently overbend as a result of incorrect early training. Very often this happens when an inexperienced horse breaker is over-anxious about the position of a young horse's head and tries to force it into what he considers to be an attractive outline. Perhaps tight side reins were put onto the horse and he was left to stand in the stable or made to work on the lunge. The horse, whose mouth was likely to be very sensitive, would soon have discovered that if he bent his neck at the crest, and nodded his head inwards, the pressure could be taken from his mouth. Once he has learnt to use this resistance it is very difficult to retrain the horse not to go in an overbent position.

Another cause of overbending can be incorrect use of curb bits.

Prevention

The horse's head should not be forced into position but must be allowed to come gradually into the desired place. It is essential that the horse bends his head from the poll and not from halfway up his neck. The head carriage will improve when the horse has muscled up and learned to engage his hocks, use his quarters and lighten his forehand as impulsion is created by his trainer. This can take years to achieve as some horses mature very slowly.

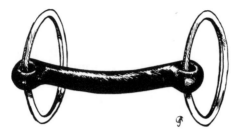

Fig. 3 Half-moon bit.

Dealing with the problem

Overbending is one of the most difficult problems to cure.

It is usually a good plan to bit the horse as lightly as possible so that his need to resist is lessened. A rubber, leather or vulcanite half-moon bit (see Fig. 3) is sometimes effective. Minimum use of the hands and maximum

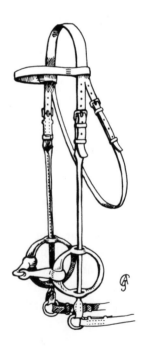

Fig. 4 Gag snaffle.

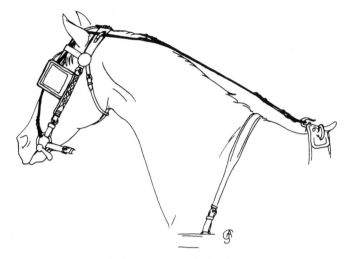

Fig. 5 Overhead check.

use of the seat and legs must be employed to slow down or stop such a horse.

A gag snaffle (see Fig. 4) is a very severe bit indeed, but it is sometimes useful to raise the head of a horse who overbends to take charge in earnest.

A driven horse can be prevented from overbending by the addition of an overhead check (see Fig. 5).

Star-gazing

Horses which star-gaze (proceed with their heads in the air) are unpleasant to ride or drive. Horses which are ewe-necked are generally more inclined to star-gaze than those with correctly shaped necks. When the rider or driver tries to check the pace the horse immediately resists by putting his head up so that his face is virtually horizontal. The pressure of the bit is moved and the horse becomes very difficult to control. The neckline is inverted so that the outline is concave at the top. This is usually accompanied by a hollow back and trailing hocks. The resistance makes the horse very uncomfortable to himself as well as to his rider or driver. He is unlikely to give a good performance in any sphere if he goes in this way. If he is being jumped, he will not round his back and will probably drag his legs through fences. If he is inclined to take charge of his rider or driver it will be found that he will be very difficult to stop once he gets his head in the air.

Cause

Horses usually star-gaze because they are unhappy in their mouths or backs. Some horses have exceptionally sensitive or fleshy tongues and cannot stand the pressure of a straight or jointed bit, so they raise their heads to relieve the pain by placing the bit in a different position.

A rough rider or driver who hangs onto a horse with a sensitive mouth, can make the horse star-gaze.

An ill-fitting saddle can cause a horse to fuss with his head if his back is hurting.

Prevention

Care must be taken to ensure that the horse is bitted correctly so that he is comfortable in his mouth. A horse with a sensitive or fleshy tongue will probably prefer to wear a bit with a low port (see Figs. 6 (opposite) and 10 (page 56)). The tongue can then fit snugly into the curve of the bit and the pressure will be transferred to the bars of the mouth.

Fig. 6 Low port mouth-piece on a Kimblewick bit.

Dealing with the problem

Groundwork, on the circle on long reins, with the horse in a comfortable bit, is an effective way of correcting horses who proceed with their heads in the air. It is essential that obedience to the voice is obtained, on the circle, on the lunge, before the horse is long-reined. The horse can then be controlled initially, with a minimum of pressure on his mouth, from the long reins, and resistances, such as star-gazing, are avoided. The horse's head must not be pulled into place but encouraged into a position where he will discover that he is most comfortable. As the horse gains confidence in his bitting, stronger contact can be taken on his mouth. If the horse is required for such work as ridden dressage tests he can be worked under saddle when the rider's legs and seat can be used instead of the voice. Driven horses can of course be controlled considerably by the voice as this, thankfully, is permitted in driven dressage competitions.

When the ridden horse is worked on long reins, a driving saddle can be placed on top of a riding saddle and girthed up around the saddle girth (see Fig. 7). This method prevents the use of a crupper which can cause considerable trouble to a horse who is not accustomed to such equipment. The dip in the seat of the saddle prevents the driving saddle from being pulled forward

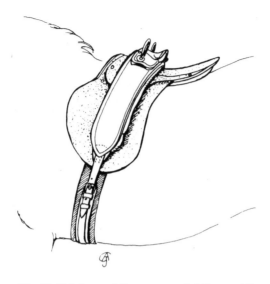

Fig. 7 Driving saddle on top of riding saddle.

towards the horse's withers. A driving saddle which is used without a crupper will slip forward if it is not placed on top of a riding saddle. The reins, which should be light to prevent overbending, are buckled onto the bit on each side of the horse's mouth and passed through the terrets on the driving saddle before going back to the trainer's hands.

Long-reining is a difficult and highly skilled art. If it is practised by an expert it is, without doubt, the simplest way of correcting this particular head problem.

The horse should be worked at a slow, rhythmic trot, being sent forward with plenty of impulsion, which is created by the voice and by the lunge whip pointing towards the hindquarters. The trainer must follow through with a very light and steady feeling on the reins. The weight of the reins, as they hang in a slight loop, will usually give enough contact. Beginners experience great difficulty in maintaining a steady feeling between their hands and their horse's mouth. It should be remembered that the inner rein controls the bend and the outer rein controls the pace. The position of the trainer, in relation to the horse, is the secret of success. The trainer should remain slightly towards the horse's quarters so that he is able to send the horse forward. If the trainer gets in front of the horse, the pupil is almost certain to stop and swing round to face his trainer..

Carefully planned training with long reins will probably cure a star-gazer. Over a period of several months, the muscles on the underneath of the neck can be reduced and those on the top of the neck can be built up so that the horse's outline will change. Providing that he is bitted and worked carefully and correctly the problem should be reduced considerably if not eliminated.

A method of schooling a horse who star-gazes when he is being driven is to buckle a pair of lunge reins onto the shaft tugs and pass them through the rings of the bit before running them back through the saddle terrets to the driver's hands (see Fig. 8). If the horse resists by putting his head up when the driver puts contact onto his mouth through the driving reins, then his head can be brought down with the lunge reins. Great care must be taken to ensure that the lunge reins run freely. The method can be dangerous if a rein becomes caught in any way, such as round a shaft tip.

A similar method can be employed for work on the circle when the horse is long-reined. The buckle ends of the lunge reins can be secured to the tops of the driving saddle girth points before being passed through the bit rings and driving saddle terrets to the driver's hands. This is, of course, very severe and should only be used in extreme cases. Unless extra-long lunge reins are used it will be found necessary to have extensions of about 6 feet (2 metres) at the hand end. It is not a good idea to extend the lunge reins at the buckle end because the weight of the buckle and swivel will be found to cause too much contact if they are joined to extensions near the horse's mouth or the saddle terrets. It is essential that a light and sympathetic contact is maintained if this method is used.

A horse can be ridden with a similar device by putting a second pair of reins with webbing extensions from the saddle girth, through the bit rings, to the rider's hands. Care must be taken if this method is employed not to force the horse's head down so that his stride is shortened

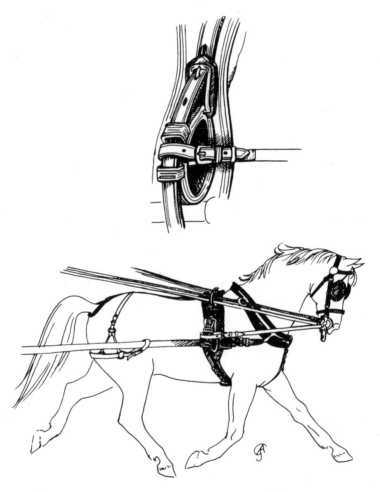

Fig. 8 A method of correcting a star-gazer in harness.

and he becomes overbent. If he is pulled forcibly into position, instead of being pushed into place from increased use of his hindquarters, the horse will probably become heavy in his forehand and his stride and paces will be ruined.

Some people use artificial aids such as standing martingales and tight side reins. These are sometimes effective when they are on the horse but he will probably revert to his previous way of going once his head is released.

Toe Dragging and Stumbling

Horses who drag their hind feet with almost every trotting stride are a nuisance because they quickly wear out their back shoes at the toe, whilst the rest of the shoe remains relatively unworn. The shoes become thin at the front and then break in half and twist to one side of the foot. The inner heel is likely to strike the opposite fetlock causing damage to the joint.

Some horses stumble over their front feet and may come down onto their knees. This is exceedingly dangerous for a rider, who is likely to get thrown over the animal's head and may receive serious injuries. Driven horses who are inclined to stumbling are even more dangerous. If such a horse is in single harness, the driver and passenger could be pitched off their seats as the shafts are suddenly lowered to the road when the horse falls.

A horse with scarred knees is labelled for life as a stumbler and should be viewed with suspicion. Contrary to reassurances from vendors it is unlikely that all horses with broken knees have incurred their blemishes by 'hitting a stone wall out hunting'.

Cause

Lack of impulsion is frequently the cause of both habits. If the horse was not trained correctly to use his hocks when he was broken, he may go through life dragging his back legs and wearing out the toes of his hind shoes.

Stumbling can be caused by the horse being physically incapable of the work which is required of him. He may be unfit and not able to carry, or pull, the weight which is asked. If young horses are forced to do too much work, before their muscles have had time to develop, they may stumble or drag their feet.

A faulty blood condition (such as anaemia) can cause the problem, as can excessive worms or unsoundness.

Prevention

When a horse is broken he must be encouraged to use his hocks. He will develop the correct muscles and his forehand will automatically lighten. He will then neither drag his toes nor stumble.

Work over poles is an effective exercise for a young horse on the lunge. Six solid poles should be placed on the ground at intervals of about 4 feet 6 inches (1.4

metres) for a 14 h.h. pony. They should be widened for a longer-striding horse and placed nearer together for a short-striding pony. It is best to use square or half-round poles which are heavy and about 15 feet (4.5 metres) long. Obviously training must begin with a single pole, increasing to six when the horse is confident. They should be put alongside a hedge or fence to form as near to a straight line as possible on a circle which is at least 60 feet (18 metres) in diameter.

The horse should be worked at the trot with a slow and even rhythm. It is often a help if the trainer hums a two-beat tune to himself in order to keep the horse to a strict tempo. This will ensure that he does not rush, or slow down, as he goes over the poles. He should step with alternate feet over each pole. It will be noticed that the hocks will bend more acutely and be put to greater use as the horse goes over the poles. Impulsion is increased naturally and muscles will be developed without difficulty. The horse will also learn to co-ordinate his hind feet with his front ones.

As he learns to use his hindquarters, his forehand will automatically lighten and his head will naturally come into the correct place.

Dealing with the problem

If a horse persistently stumbles or drags his hind feet it is probably best to seek veterinary advice.

Assuming that the animal is physically fit, then the work which is described above should be carried out and will probably be found to be helpful.

Some horses need to be given more oats to increase their energy.

When they are ridden or driven, they must be kept up to their bridles and not allowed by a lazy or careless horseman to slop along.

It is a good idea to discuss the problem with the farrier who will probably have experienced similar cases and will be able to advise special shoeing. Rolled toes are frequently used for both cases. A rolled toe in place of a front toe clip is often helpful for a horse which stumbles. A rolled toe with a hardener added, lessens the speed at which a toe dragger goes through his hind shoes.

Catching Hold of a Running Martingale

It is mostly young horses who catch hold of the branches of a running martingale although once they have developed the habit they may continue to practise it for the rest of their lives. They learn to duck their heads to one side and grab the piece of leather which goes from the neckstrap to the rein. This is very dangerous because if the martingale strap gets caught on a corner incisor, or tush in the case of an older horse, he may be forced sideways and backwards. He could perhaps rear and fall onto his unfortunate rider, who will have been powerless to release the horse from his self-imposed predicament.

Cause

The desire of a young horse to grab onto any available object when he is teething, is likely to be the initial cause of this habit.

Prevention

It is safest not to ride in the conventional type of running martingale if the horse is known to get hold of it. An Irish martingale (see Fig. 9) may be preferable if the

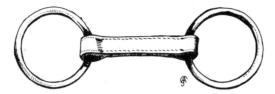

Fig. 9 Irish martingale.

sole reason for the running martingale is to keep the reins on either side of the young horse's neck when he swings his head about.

Dealing with the problem

If the horse has to be ridden in a running martingale then it is safest to use one which is made with a triangle of leather between the two straps which go from the neckstrap to the reins. The horse will not be able to get his mouth caught. This type of martingale is known as a bib martingale and can be obtained from any good saddler.

Grabbing the Cheek of a Bit

Some horses discover how to grab the cheek of their curb bit with the side of the mouth. It is annoying because the driver's or rider's control is lessened until the cheek has been pulled away from the lips or corner incisors. It also results in the horse being unsteady in his mouth and will probably lead to head problems. The habit can encourage rein chewing.

Cause

The problem is usually caused, like so many of this type, by the desire of the young horse to hold something between his teeth when he is suffering the teething stage of his early life.

Prevention

If the habit is not stopped immediately, by taking preventative measures, he may continue to catch hold of the cheek of his bit and it might become established. The simplest method is to use a bit which does not have cheek-pieces. It is unlikely that the young horse will be worked in a severe curb so the trainer might just as well use a ring snaffle with a mouth-piece which is suitable for the horse concerned. If a slight curb action is required then a Kimblewick (see Fig. 6, page 47) serves the purpose without having to have cheeks which the horse can grab. This avoids using cheeked bits whilst the horse is teething. It will probably be found that once he has

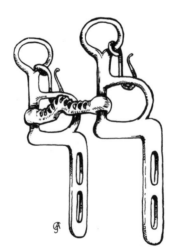

Fig. 10 Elbow bit with low port mouth-piece.

outgrown the tendency he can be ridden or driven in a cheeked curb bit without any problem.

Dealing with the problem

If the horse has to be ridden or driven in a curb bit then an Elbow bit (see Fig. 10) is ideal. This is also known as an Army Reversible bit because the mouth-piece is rough on one side and plain on the other so that it can be used according to the severity required. It is designed specifically to overcome the problem of cheek grabbing and is so shaped that the horse cannot get hold of the cheek between his lips. It also makes it harder for a horse to chew his reins.

This bit is quite acceptable for showing a horse in harness.

Head Shaking

Horses who persistently shake their heads cause grave concern to riders or drivers who are trying to train them to perform correctly.

Cause

The possible causes of head shaking are numerous. The trouble may be in the horse's mouth, nose or ears. It can even be caused, in the case of a harness horse, by aching neck muscles or sore shoulders. Twisting of the head can be caused by a spinal injury.

An ill fitting bridle can make a horse very uncomfortable. If the browband is too short, the head-piece will be pulled forward and forced against the base of the ears. This will cause considerable discomfort and applies more to driving or in-hand bridles which have brass rosettes on the browband.

A bit which is too wide or too narrow can make a horse miserable. If his tongue is being pinched he is likely to throw his head about in order to relieve the pressure.

Young horses, between the ages of three and five years, can suffer considerable discomfort when they are teething. They frequently have inflamed gums where new teeth are forcing their way alongside milk teeth. Loose molars almost certainly cause some pain.

The presence of wolf teeth, which sometimes appear alongside the fronts of the molars, can create head shaking.

A few animals suffer from pollen or similar allergies between April and September, causing sneezing and discomfort on dry, sunny days. Such animals usually keep their heads still on wet days.

It is possible for a horse to shake his head and drop one ear sideways to convince his owner that the problem is serious when in fact the cause is entirely from irritation by sweat around the ears. This is more likely to occur in the spring, when the animal is changing his coat, than in the summer or winter.

Prevention

It is essential to ensure that the bridle fits correctly in every detail so that irritations are not caused by carelessness. It is also important to see that the horse is bitted to his satisfaction. Some horses will not tolerate a jointed bit. Many prefer a half-moon or low-port mouth-piece to accommodate their tongue. Extremely sensitive animals may prefer rubber, vulcanite, or leather mouthpieces to those which are made of metal.

Dealing with the problem

If all the above suggestions have been attended to and head shaking persists, it is best to get the advice of a veterinary surgeon. He will inspect the horse's mouth for wolf teeth. These can be removed if necessary. He will shine a specially bright light up the animal's nostrils to check for inflammation or swelling. The animals ears will also be examined with a light and excess wax can be removed.

If the animal is shaking because of irritation caused by a correctly fitting browband and rosettes, it can be a help to keep these permanently on the horse's headcollar which is worn day and night. The animal may then learn to accept this pressure and cease to shake.

Tongue over the Bit

A horse or pony which gets its tongue over the bit can become difficult to control. It usually results in him throwing his head about or dropping the bit in an effort to get his tongue back underneath the bit. The driver or rider will find that the horse becomes very unsettled in his work and will not concentrate.

Cause

This fault is usually due to careless early training. The habit is frequently caused initially by the bit being placed too low in the horse's mouth. The horse then accidently gets his tongue over the bit. Once the habit is formed it can be hard to cure. Too wide a jointed bit can also result in the tongue being brought over the centre joint which may be lying almost on top of the central incisors. A horse with a very sensitive or fleshy tongue may put it on top of the bit in order to relieve the pressure.

Prevention

It is a good idea when mouthing a horse in the early stages of training, to use a straight-bar tongue-plated bit (see Fig. 11). This enables the bit to be left at a comfortable height in the animal's mouth. Young horses frequently get their tongues over jointed mouthing bits unless they are placed very high. This often results in the corners of the lips becoming sore which makes matters worse.

It is essential to act immediately if a horse is seen to put his tongue over the bit. The habit must not be ignored in the hope that it will go away.

If the horse has a sensitive tongue it is often a help to use a bit which has a low port (see Figs. 6 (page 47) and 10 (page 56)) so that the pressure is taken off the centre of the tongue and transferred to the bars of the mouth.

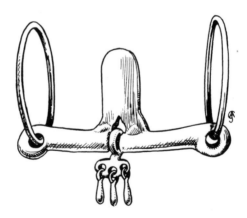

Fig. 11 Straight-bar tongue-plated mouthing bit.

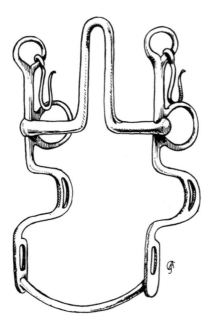

Fig. 12 High ported bit.

Bits with very high ports (see Fig. 12) were made to prevent this problem. They have the disadvantage in that if they are used in conjunction with a curb rein they press against the roof of the mouth and cause a lot of pain. This, of course, was fully intended when they were designed at the turn of the nineteenth century for hard-mouthed coach and riding horses.

Dealing with the problem

It is possible to buy quite cheaply a rubber tongue plate (see Fig. 13) from a saddler's shop. This can easily be threaded around the mouth-piece of a bit to prevent the horse from getting his tongue over the top. It is mild and effective. It lies gently on top of the tongue and

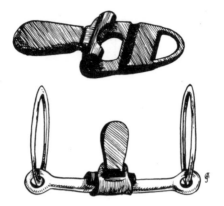

Fig. 13 Tongue plate and its fitting on bit.

most horses accept its presence. The bit can be kept at a comfortable height in the mouth and the horse will be happy in his work.

Napping

Nappy horses resist by jibbing, rearing, running back, lying down and bucking. All are described in the following sections under those headings.

Jibbing

A horse is said to 'jib' if he refuses to go forward in the required direction. In fact, a serious and confirmed jibber is likely to refuse to go in any direction, forwards, backwards or sideways. Jibbing frequently leads to rearing. It can even result in the animal lying down as a final and definite resistance to the rider's or driver's demands. Broken saddles, harness and carts are the product of such a habit.

Cause

Jibbing is usually caused initially by mismanagement.

When a horse is being broken it is essential that the trainer should foresee a situation which might result in jibbing and take avoiding action. If, for instance, a horse who is new to work in harness is asked to pull too heavy a load on the level, or a light load up a steep hill, he may stop because he finds that he cannot haul such a weight with shoulders which are unmuscled or perhaps a little sore. Once the horse has discovered that he can avoid the work by merely refusing to go forward, or even lying down, he may develop the habit.

A ridden horse might be afraid of such a simple matter as stepping over a puddle or walking through a slightly overgrown gap in a pathway. If he discovers that by stopping, and refusing to go forward, his rider will give way he immediately learns that he can use his strength to get the better of his rider. He may then develop the habit so that eventually he will refuse to do anything that he does not want to do. In a short time it will probably be impossible to take him anywhere with confidence.

It is a known fact that a horse who has originally shied away from a white gate in a hedge is quite likely to shy at the same place, if passed on daily exercise, for years even though the gate may have become rotten and green with age. The habit of shying has become established.

The same applies to a horse which has been allowed to jib. If he once finds that he can stop at a certain place he is likely to continue the habit even if the original reason is removed.

It is a grave error to take a young horse on the same route each day. When the time comes to go a different way he may refuse because he is afraid of that which is unfamiliar. Equally, the horse should never be taken down a road and turned round and brought back. He will soon anticipate the turn and may jib if he is asked to go further. He may eventually stop before he gets to the turning point in his desire to go home. It may not be long before he will not leave his stable yard without a scene.

Prevention

The harness horse must not be asked to pull heavy loads until he has learnt obedience and his shoulders are sufficiently muscled to enable him to carry out his job in comfort. He should be fully prepared both mentally and physically to fulfil the work which is required of him.

The ridden horse must be prepared in a similar way. Care should be taken not to ask a question unless the right answer is likely to be given. If, for instance, there are known 'horrors' on a ride, then it is wise to take the young horse out with a schoolmaster ridden by another person. The youngster can be tucked in alongside the mature horse and he will probably follow the calm example. Trouble will be avoided and jibbing will not occur. Eventually the young horse can be ridden alone and will not be afraid; he will face the 'horrors' which might have initially caused jibbing.

Ideally, the horse should always be taken on a circuitous route or at least to a convenient turning point, such as a village green, which can be ridden or driven round.

Dealing with the problem

Confirmed elderly jibbers are hard to cure.

One doubtful method which came to the author's

ears some time ago tells of a harness horse who refused to go forward when put to his gig. His desperate driver lit a fire under the horse who in retaliation walked forward just far enough to place his gig over the fire!

Once a single harness horse has acquired the habit of jibbing and lying down there is little that can be done. The horse is never likely to be reliable as he may resort to the resistance whenever he wishes to evade his driver.

When horses were used in earnest such an animal would probably have been put into the wheel of a team. Then, when he lay down, the other three horses would have been driven on to drag the offender along until he scrambled to his feet. Presumably, this taught him a lesson which he would not forget in a hurry.

The best method of dealing with a single horse which jibs is for the passenger to dismount from the carriage if all efforts of the driver to persuade him to go forward with the voice and whip have failed. The passenger should go to rear of the side of the wheel and rotate it forwards by the spokes. Quite often it will be found that once the vehicle is pushed towards the horse and the weight is removed from his shoulders he will be prepared to move on. It may be necessary for the driver also to dismount in order to go to the horse's head to lead him forward. The driver should hold the reins at their hand parts throughout this manoeuvre as well as taking hold of the piece of rein which is nearest to the horse's head. A jibbing horse is likely to plunge forward when he is moved off and may snatch the rein from the trainer's hand. The horse would then be free to get away if the trainer did not have control by the hand part of the reins. It is sometimes preferable to move the horse slightly to one side in order to start him if he is jibbing. Often, if one front foot can be moved sideways the horse will step forward with the other front foot and continue forward. Once he is going onward the driver should mount without stopping him. If he is halted he may be reluctant to go forward again. It is often wisest to leave the passenger on the ground to push the vehicle if the horse should hesitate again, until the moment of jibbing has passed.

The passenger can eventually mount and the same applies as when the driver mounted, in that the horse should not be halted.

Ridden horses who jib may only try the resistance with a weak or nervous rider. It is likely that if they are ridden by an experienced and strong horseman who forces them forward that they soon give up trying to resist.

If a ridden horse stops it is easier and more effective to persuade him to move off sideways than immediately forward. Very often, the horse will brace his front legs rigidly, slightly apart. It is best to rock him to one side with an open rein, and a tap on the shoulder with a stick, in order to get one leg moving to one side. Once he has moved one foot, he is more likely to go forward. Another gambit which sometimes works is to turn the horse in a few tight circles. He will become slightly dizzy and then may go forward, when asked, before he thinks to resist.

If this kind of method is anticipated, it is preferable to use a cheek-piece snaffle as one with small circular rings may get pulled through the horse's mouth with the sideways tension. The cheeks will make it easier to bring the horse round as they will press against the side of his face.

Rearing

Rearing is one of the most dangerous vices that a horse can have. Once he has discovered how effective it can be when he stands on his hind legs and waves his front feet in the air he may use the resistance whenever he does not wish to obey the demands of his rider or driver. The greatest danger of this vice is the risk of him coming over backwards, on top of his rider. Confirmed rearers are almost impossible to cure.

Cause

Everything said in the section on jibbing (page 62) applies to rearing. In fact, once a horse jibs, he is very likely to rear.

Prevention

Again, that which has been written regarding jibbing also relates to rearing. It is essential that the horse should never discover how effective it is to evade his trainer in this way.

Dealing with the problem

If the horse is being ridden, great care must be taken not to pull him over backwards if he rears. The rider must immediately lean forwards, up the horse's neck, giving him a loose rein. As the horse comes down, it is best to swing him round in small circles before asking him to go forward. He should be pulled round tightly a few times and then immediately be sent on. If he rears again, it is a good idea to rotate him in the opposite direction in several tight circles before trying again to go forward. Usually, if the rider persists, the horse will eventually give in.

Some people advocate the use of a bottle of water which they say should be smashed over the top of the horse's head when he rears so that the water trickles down the animal's face making him think that it is blood. The author has never carried out such an experiment feeling that it would be difficult to cope with a bottle of water at the same time as a rearing horse! Probably either she or the horse would end up with a severe cut which would only add to the problems, or perhaps the bottle would refuse to smash anyway.

If a harness horse is known to rear in single harness then it is advisable to fasten the bellyband tighter than usual. If the bellyband is left at its normal fitting and the horse rears, he is likely to come down with the shafts across his back. If this happens, the bellyband must be unbuckled and the horse's quarters pushed back between the shafts.

If the horse is rearing as a resistance when he is being worked on long reins or the lunge it is sometimes a good idea to pull him over backwards. Very often the horse can be got off balance quite easily and a pull in the right direction will sweep him off his feet. He will not like this very much and it may act as a deterrent to future rearing. The danger of such treatment is that it could result in injury to the horse so unless the trainer is certain that he is dealing with a true rearer it is best not to resort to such violence. Some young horses will rear occasionally but once they find that it has no effect in getting them their own way they will desist. It would therefore be a great mistake to risk damaging such a horse by pulling him over.

Running Back

Horses who run backwards, as a resistance, can cause havoc and create great difficulties for their riders or drivers. It is an effective evasion which is hard to cure once the horse has fully realized his strength in the situation.

Cause

Some horses run back when they are refusing to obey the wishes of their rider or driver to go forward. The situation may be as simple as a marked reluctance to leave the stable yard. It could be caused by fear of facing up to an object of which the animal is nervous. The horse will probably begin by standing still with his feet dug firmly into the ground. Resistance to his handler's strong demands to go forward may be met by running back, rearing, whipping round or lying down.

Running back is usually initially caused by the fact that the horse was trained to rein-back too soon in his life. He must be taught to go forward, under all circumstances, before he is ever introduced to reining back.

Prevention

If a young horse is not trained to rein-back until he is about four years old, there is a good chance that it will never occur to him to use this as a method of evasion.

There is never any difficulty in teaching a horse, at four, to rein-back. By this time, if he has been carefully broken, he should be going forward correctly and will easily learn to step back when required.

It will also be found that it will be much easier to teach a horse to halt correctly, on the bit, if he has not been trained to rein-back too soon. Young horses can become very confused when they are asked to halt on the bit. They become muddled and are not certain whether or not they are meant to step back. This applies more to harness horses who cannot be held in a forward position, by leg aids, as can a ridden horse.

The simplest way of dealing with a ridden horse who runs back is to try to steer him, when he resists, so that his hindquarters contact a solid or prickly object or his hind feet drop towards a ditch. This usually has the effect of sending him sharply forward. However, it is not always easy because many horses are far too clever to allow themselves to be placed in such a situation. If there is no object suitable towards which to steer the horse's hindquarters, it can be effective to point his rear end into the desired direction for a little while so that the horse is, in fact, being made to go the right way, although backwards. He can then be turned round and will probably go forward because he may, by then, have passed the object which was causing the problem.

A harness horse who steps back must be driven forward with the whip. Work in a pair, alongside a school-master, should help to cure the culprit who will get pulled forward whether he likes it or not.

If a ridden horse is known to run back at certain places because of a reluctance to face a situation, such as pigs in a field, it is probably best to take him out alongside a quiet ridden horse who will instil confidence into the nervous horse.

It may be a help to take him out on long reins so that he can be driven on, from behind, with a lungeing whip, if he attempts to run back.

Rolling and Lying Down

Some ponies can never resist the temptation of rolling whenever they are ridden in muddy conditions or through water. More serious offenders are horses or ponies who, when they are being ridden or driven, lie down as a firm resistance to the requirements of their handler. Such animals are extremely difficult because they probably have an ungenerous temperament and are therefore very unpleasant to ride or drive. They damage and break saddles, harness and carts when they apply their tactics.

Cause

Rolling, as opposed to lying down, is sometimes practised by long-haired ponies when they get hot and sweaty. Such an animal becomes unbearably itchy and therefore decides to roll in order to rub off some of the tickles.

Lying down is much more serious. It is usually caused initially by careless breaking. If the girth is tightened too much when it is first put onto a youngster he may plunge and throw himself down in the stable when he is moved forward. Once he has discovered the effect of the resistance he may apply this method whenever he does not wish to obey his rider or driver. Some harness horses will slow down and stop when they feel pressure on their collar if the going is deep or a hill is encountered. If such a horse is told to go on, or hit, he could decide to stop even sooner and lie down. Shafts get broken and hame and saddle terrets become bent as the horse goes onto his side.

Prevention

The ridden pony should be trace clipped, or at least have a strip down his windpipe and belly clipped out, to make him more comfortable if he is going to be worked hard when he has grown his full winter coat.

The child must be warned that his pony is likely to roll when he gets hot and sticky. He should be told to keep the pony on the move in muddy or wet conditions and particularly if the pony begins to paw the ground as this usually is a warning signal to rolling.

Care must be taken when breaking to ensure that the horse is never antagonized into lying down, by girthing too tightly, too soon, so that it never occurs to him to resist in this way.

Dealing with the problem

A child whose pony is likely to lie down must be told to hit the pony hard as soon as he begins to paw the ground and fold up. The child should be instructed to quit his stirrups and jump off quickly if the pony should succeed in lying down. He must then hit the pony hard to prevent him from rolling and breaking his saddle.

There is little that can be done with a single harness horse which lies down other than to get it up as soon as possible by which time it is likely that shafts and harness will have been damaged. Such a horse is best abandoned as far as harness work is concerned.

Bucking

Bucking is an unpleasant habit which can be embarrassing and uncomfortable if the result is a loose horse and an injured rider. It must not be tolerated because it will almost certainly lead to disaster one day.

Cause

Horses buck for a variety of reasons. Too much food and too little exercise are the most usual causes.

Some horses will give a playful buck from sheer *joie de vivre* when moving off behind a pack of hounds at the beginning of the day. Such bucks are usually relatively harmless and are often caused by a feeling, shared by the rider, of excited anticipation of the day's sport.

More serious bucks are those which are caused by the horse wishing to dispose of his rider. The horse perhaps resents the presence of someone on his back. He resists by arching his spine upwards and putting his head between his knees so that he is able to proceed in a series of stiff-legged bounds with his hind legs flying out backwards at each stride, until he finally dislodges his unfortunate passenger.

Once he has learnt how effective this can be, he will probably repeat the performance and add a dropped shoulder for good measure.

A leather- or linen-lined saddle on a cold-backed horse can result in bucking.

An ill-fitting saddle which pinches or presses on the horse's back, or spine, can also make him buck.

Mischievous children think that it is fun to make a pony buck by placing their hands on the animal's loins when they are riding. This must be discouraged at all costs.

Prevention

Some young horses are initially made to buck by a careless trainer who buckles the girth too tightly to begin with.

It is a great mistake when a youngster is first backed (ridden), to apply the legs strongly to get him to go forward. In all probability he will not know what is desired of him. A young horse will almost certainly stiffen his back and legs in resistance to pressure from the rider's legs. If the rider persists by using his heels against the horse's ribs, or a whip on the hindquarters, the horse will probably jump forward and perhaps buck when he feels the rider's weight move in the saddle. This might dislodge the rider; the horse has learnt how easy it is to get rid of his passenger and the problem has begun.

The rider should persuade the horse quietly forward with his voice and it is sometimes a help to tap the horse on the shoulder, or either side of the wither, with the end of the rein. Also, the horse can usually be moved off by being brought slightly sideways with an open rein. This rather unorthodox method will probably get the horse to move forward without the risk of his back going up at this early stage of being ridden. Of course, after a couple of days, once the horse has got used to the idea of someone on his back, light leg aids can be used to teach the horse to obey the rider's legs.

An older horse who is used to being ridden can usually be prevented from bucking by the rider's anticipation of the situation. This vice is most likely to occur when the horse is on grass at a time when he is going to be asked to canter. It is essential to hold his head up and keep him balanced and in full control so that he is held between hand and leg. Any attempt to buck must be immediately dealt with by a sharp reprimand. The whip, if used, must be employed on the shoulder rather than behind the girth.

Dealing with the problem

If the horse is known to be cold-backed it is wise to put a sheepskin numnah under the saddle. It is also a good idea to saddle up for at least fifteen minutes before mounting to give the horse time to warm up the saddle.

It is essential to ensure that the saddle is not pinching the withers or pressing on the backbone and that the girth is not pinching any skin at the base of the saddle.

Bucking must be severely discouraged. The habit may begin in a light-hearted way but it can quickly develop into a vice. If the horse is going to buck he will put his head down in order to get his hind legs up. The rider must keep the horse's head up and at the same time send the horse forward. It will be difficult for him to buck severely if he is sent onwards and his head is kept up. A firm command of the situation and punishment from the rider, such as a jerk in the mouth, accompanied by a strong vocal reprimand, will probably discourage the horse from bucking.

Some riders prefer to stand in their stirrups and let the motion go on underneath as they peg themselves firmly to the saddle with the sides and fronts of their knees. They claim that the bucks will be far less unseating than if they try to remain in the seat of the saddle. Other riders prefer to sit down firmly into the depth of the saddle in order to drive the horse forward. Both methods can be effective. Whichever is chosen, however, must lead to the horse being strongly corrected and being hit sharply down the shoulder. He will probably desist once he realizes that he will be punished.

A jointed bit, which works on the corners of the mouth, is best for raising the horse's head. A plain snaffle, for a horse with a reasonable mouth, or a gag snaffle for a hard-mouthed horse, will probably keep his head up.

Running Away ('Bolting')

The word 'bolting' is frequently used by inexperienced people who are inclined to say that a horse bolted with them when in fact he perhaps merely cantered up to the field gate and the rider, owing to his incompetence, was unable to stop. Serious runaways are quite different. It is extremely unpleasant to be carted by a horse who is determined to ignore his rider's demands to reduce pace. A harness horse, taking off, is one of the most frightening situations which can ever be experienced in driving.

Cause

There are numerous causes of a horse running away. The situation is usually created by fear. The horse may have seen or heard something which has frightened him. Flight is the horse's main defence and he naturally resorts to this means of escape. A donkey or pig, standing innocently in a roadside field, can cause a horse to take off smartly in the opposite direction if he is afraid of such animals.

Noise from behind can frighten a harness horse, even more than a ridden horse, as he will probably be wearing blinkers and will not be able to see that which he can hear. If the noise is being created by the cart, he will go even faster as he finds that the cart appears to be chasing him.

Numerous accidents are caused by people who remove a blinkered bridle from a harness horse whilst he is still between the shafts. If the horse has not been used to being driven in an open bridle, he is almost certain to take off. This can apply to the quietest of horses. If he steps forward, he will see the wheels of the vehicle turning with the tops appearing to catch up with him. He will probably then increase his pace to get away from the cart which he thinks is chasing him. It is only a matter of seconds before he has galloped off. He will probably keep going until the cart hits something and smashes into pieces. The horse is likely to be ruined for life as far as work in harness is concerned, because it is unlikely that he will ever forget his terrible fright. Although he may emerge from the wreckage physically unharmed, the mental damage will last for ever.

Prevention

A horse must not be allowed to run away. The rider or driver should always pay attention to his animal and take immediate action if there is any question of the horse getting out of control.

Care should be taken with the amount of corn which is fed so that the horse is not given more than he can comfortably take to remain sensible. This especially applies to periods before he is to be ridden, or driven, in company, when the sights and sounds of other horses will inevitably excite him. He may then try to gallop off in his enthusiasm. Adequate exercise is also very important.

Care must be taken to ensure that he is correctly bitted. If the horse is known to be likely to catch hold, it is sensible to bit him adequately so that he can be kept under full control. It is no earthly use taking him out hunting in a rubber snaffle if, when at home, he can barely be checked in this mild bit. Riding a horse, so bitted, if he decides to take charge, can be rather like riding with a headcollar.

A harness horse who is accustomed to wearing a Liverpool bit with the rein on plain cheek (see Fig. 14) should perhaps have the rein put onto the rough cheek position (see Fig. 15) when he is first taken out in company so that stronger control can be achieved if necessary.

Dealing with the problem

If a ridden horse should manage to get away with his rider, there are various ways of pulling up. On no account should the rider try to jump off. He is almost certain to get injured and is far less likely to be hurt if he stays with his horse.

The first thing to remember is that it does not do much good to lean forward and take a steady pull. The horse has probably crossed and set his jaw and will not

Fig. 14 Liverpool bit with the rein buckled to plain cheek.

Fig. 15 Liverpool bit with the rein buckled to rough cheek.

pay any attention to a dead pull. His neck, after all, is considerably stronger than his rider's arms. The best method is to pin the knees firmly to the saddle and straighten one arm so that the hand can be pressed firmly on the horse's wither, with a tight rein. The other hand then takes an equally tight rein and works in a series of strong, even, pulls on one side of the horse's mouth. This has a very severe effect on the tongue and corners of the lips on one side, particularly in a jointed bit, and will probably check the horse.

Sawing at the mouth, from one side to the other, can be effective but the rider cannot be as still or steady with this as with the one-arm method when he can sit very quietly whilst dealing with the situation.

If the horse is being ridden in a field then he can be circled in order to check the pace. He can be pulled round in a very large circle to begin with, and gradually the circles can be reduced until the horse has stopped. If this tactic is likely to be necessary it is best to ride the horse in a cheek piece or very large-ringed snaffle because a small-ringed bit will get pulled through his mouth.

If there is a convenient steep hill nearby, it helps to take the horse up this incline on which it will be far easier to check.

The main secret of stopping a runaway is to keep calm and react quickly. The longer he is allowed to go, before he is checked, the more difficult he will be to stop.

Of course, the exception to this would be if space were unlimited which, in England, is unlikely. If he is being ridden in open acreage then he can be allowed to gallop on and on. Then, when he checks of his own accord he must be made to continue until his rider decides, eventually, to pull him up. He will then be only too relieved to stop.

A harness horse which gallops off causes a far more serious problem than does a ridden horse. The driver cannot circle for fear of turning the carriage over. His only hope is to sit tight, take a rein in each hand, and saw the horse's mouth from side to side as hard as he can. It is amazing how, on the few occasions that the writer has experienced this very unpleasant situation, sawing has been effective in checking the horse from his furious pace. On no account must a driver jump from the cart. He will almost surely get badly hurt.

The main cure for a harness horse is prevention. He must not be allowed to get out of hand. Galloping in harness can be disastrous and should be firmly restricted to very experienced people who practise the art when competing against the clock at events or in scurry-driving contests.

If a horse is a confirmed runaway he should *never* be driven.

Kicking

Horses who kick seriously are dangerous. They are a menace out hunting, unreliable in harness and unpleasant in the stable.

Cause

Some horses, for no apparent reason, appear to be more prone to kicking than others. Stallions rarely kick, preferring to use their teeth and front legs as a defence. Mares, particularly when they are in season, are perhaps more inclined, in general, to kick than geldings.

Prevention

It is very hard to prevent horses who instinctively kick,

from doing so. No doubt severe correction in the form-
ative years is a help but will not necessarily be effective.
When riding in company, the horse should be held well
together whenever anyone rides too closely behind, and
it may then be possible to divert him from kicking.

It is a good idea, when hunting a young horse for the
first few times, to put a green ribbon (meaning 'green
horse') on the top of his tail to discourage people from
riding too close and maybe causing an otherwise innocent
horse to kick.

Dealing with the problem

Kicking is very difficult to cure. It is a natural reaction
which some horses apply as a means of defence and
therefore almost impossible to eradicate from those who
practise this disagreeable habit.

The only possible hope of curing a kicker is to punish
him strongly the moment he attempts to kick. He must
be made to realize, right from the start, that kicking will
not be tolerated. He may decide that it is preferable to
contain his wrath than receive severe and painful punishment from his trainer.

It is difficult to punish harness horses who kick once
they are between shafts or alongside a pole. Hitting will
probably make them kick harder. A severe jab in the
mouth is the only hope. Once a hind leg has made contact
with the splinter bar or dashboard the wood soon starts
to disintegrate. The kicking usually continues until
contact may be made with the driver and passenger,
who are literally sitting targets for the battering. Inveter-
ate kickers should not be driven.

Kicking straps are said to hold the horse's quarters
down and may deter a mild kicker. They do not, however, prevent a violent and determined kicker.

One method, which was used by some nineteenth-
century trainers, was to put the animal into a four-
wheeled vehicle, so that the driver and passenger were

not tipped out, and to pull the kicker down onto his knees when he started to kick. Separate hobbles were put around each front pastern. A rope was fixed to the back of each hobble. The ropes were then passed through a ring on the girth and up to the assistant alongside the driver. When the horse began to kick, the ropes were pulled and the horse was brought smartly to his knees. This treatment has never been practised by the writer and it is not recommended.

If a kicker has to be ridden in company then pride must be swallowed and a large red ribbon must be tied, firmly, to the top of the animal's tail. This acts as a warning signal to fellow riders. A red ribbon must *not* be used as a passport to riding at the front. It is quite wrong to expect everyone to give way to such a horse in fear of being kicked. Horses who are adorned with red ribbons should be kept right away from crowded areas.

A kicking horse in the stable should be fed by the door so that the feeder does not have to walk out past the hind legs after the animal has been given his feed. The horse must be trained to stand at the back of the box when the feed is brought in.

It is probably best to keep a headcollar on such a horse so that he can be easily caught in his loose-box.

It can be a help to hold up a front leg to prevent the horse from kicking when it is necessary to carry out a simple job such as putting on a tail bandage, although determined kickers manage to stand on two legs, whilst one front leg is held up and they kick with the remaining leg.

Jogging

Horses who jog instead of walk can be extremely tiring to ride. Their incessant jogging shakes the rider and irritates the driver. It also often causes the animal to sweat unnecessarily and become upset. Horses who jog instead of walk on returning from a day's hunting will probably still be warm when they get back to their horsebox or stable and will be more likely to 'break out' later, than an animal who has walked home calmly.

Cause

Jogging usually develops because the horse is excited. He wants to hurry when his rider would prefer him to walk. Sometimes the habit begins because the animal is small or has a shorter stride than the horse or pony which is being ridden or driven alongside. Then, in order to keep up, he jogs.

Some horses jog because their riders encourage the habit believing that it looks rather dashing and clever.

Prevention

Jogging can usually be prevented by the trainer never permitting it. When riding, or driving, he should insist that the animal always walks.

Dealing with the problem

If a horse or pony breaks from a walk to a jog when he is being ridden, he must be quietly and firmly brought back to walk and told verbally to walk. As soon as he walks he should be given a free rein and encouraged to lower his head and lengthen his stride. He can be gently and quietly urged forward until he is walking with a regular four-time pace. He must swing along and cover the ground with ease and impulsion. His hind feet should track well beyond those of his front feet. If he breaks pace into a jog, he must be brought tactfully back with the legs, seat and hands, and told again to 'Walk'. He can then gradually be sent forward. Perseverance will eventually result in the horse walking instead of jogging although it may take a long time.

Great care has to be taken when driving, not to bring the horse back from a jog to a walk so strongly that he almost halts in his confusion at being checked. As he checks, the cart runs towards him causing the breeching to tighten. Then, if he is dropped by his driver, he may jerk forwards into his collar from a half halt which will both confuse and upset him and do nothing towards teaching him to walk instead of jog. The matter will, in fact, be worsened. Extreme cases can result in broken harness. It requires light hands, tact and skill gently to bring the horse back from a jog to a walk and then to let him forward exactly the right amount, at the right moment, so that he continues to walk on, in preference to either halting or continuing to jog. This manoeuvre is, in many ways, similar to sailing when at one point in 'going about', the helm is heavy in the hand when the sails are filled. Then, as the bows are brought round the sails slacken before being gently filled again as the boat goes off on the other tack. The same feeling of strength, followed by lightness, is experienced. It may be for this reason that people who have experience of sailing often find that driving gives a similar feeling of excitement and control.

Unusual Behaviour – A Possible Explanation

Sometimes a horse can behave in a way which appears to be quite extraordinary. He may, when loose in the field, suddenly start to gallop about frantically as though being chased. When he is ridden or driven, he might suddenly seem to go almost crazy. He will perhaps kick at his belly, jump in the air, or try to turn his head to bite at his side. His tail is likely to be swished violently.

He may, if turned out in the field, walk solemnly round in a large oval, in the evening or at sunrise, during the summer months. He will make a track to which he keeps, as he walks on and on, for an hour or longer, as though he is under some telepathic signal to keep going.

Cause

This violent behaviour is likely to be caused by a hornet, horse fly, wasp or bee. These are capable of giving a horse a painful sting and so naturally horses become terrified when they hear one buzzing around.

Persistent walking is often caused by tiny midges which can create problems for horses at grass at sunset and sunrise during the summer. They get into the animal's mane and tail and bite viciously. The horse then rubs to try to remove them and sometimes creates sores which, in turn, attract the midges. Some horses will get down into a sitting position to rub their belly against their hind fetlock to remove midges from the sensitive skin near their udder or sheath.

Prevention

It is a help to use fly spray before riding or driving during the summer if the area is noted for insects which sting or bite.

Animals who are susceptible to midges should be kept in at night so that they are not subjected to the misery of being bitten at dawn and dusk, which in the summer can mean 4.30 am and 10.00 pm, so it is not really practical to turn them out at night at that time of the year.

Dealing with the problem

Very often it is possible to dismount and swat the hornet or horse fly once the horse has made it clear that he is about to be stung.

Carters used to hang small branches of elder amongst the harness as horse flies do not like the smell of crushed elder.

Benzole Benzoate, which can be obtained from a chemist, can be rubbed into the mane, tail and belly to help an animal who has to be out at dawn and dusk during the summer.

One summer, when the midges were particularly vicious, the author's four harness ponies were seen walking round in single file, in the order in which they were driven as two tandems. Alibi led the way, followed by Razali, her sister. Next came Lorenzo who was followed by his brother, Loretto. They soon made a track round the field. Occasionally one would stop to graze or scratch but would return into its place. Needless to say, as soon as this was noticed they were brought into the stable, away from the midges, and sprayed before being kept in for the night.

Shying

Shying is a habit which can be both dangerous and irritating. It is dangerous when a horse is so occupied with shying violently from something like a paper bag in the hedge, that he does not seem to care whether or not he is likely to be hit by an oncoming lorry of which he is not the slightest bit afraid. It is irritating when the horse spends his entire time looking for things from which to shy whilst he is being ridden or driven. The rider or driver is never able to relax and the whole business of exercising becomes nerve-racking.

Cause

Some horses shy because they are really nervous of things lurking along the sides of the road. Others shy because they enjoy finding excuses to jump about. They are probably over-fed, or under exercised, or both. Some shy out of habit.

Many horses are, in fact, made to shy by their rider or driver. It is the old story of fear travelling down the reins. If the handler expects the horse to shy he may take a strong contact on the animal's mouth, the horse will presume that something is going to happen and will react accordingly. The smell of adrenalin which is given off by a nervous rider or driver, will almost certainly cause the horse to shy when he might otherwise have passed quietly by the cause of the problem if he had not been given the warning signal of apprehension from his handler.

Prevention

Genuinely nervous horses are better if they are ridden in company. Horses are, by nature, very gregarious creatures and they are great believers in safety in numbers. Nervy animals can be tucked in alongside, or behind, a non-shying schoolmaster and will probably take note of and copy his good example.

When riding or driving a horse who is likely to shy it is essential to inspire the animal with confidence. If he should start to look at something of which he is obviously afraid it is often a help to talk him by the horror with a calm voice. It is important to leave the reins as slack as possible. He must not be hit, as this will make him even more afraid.

Dealing with the problem

When a horse shies, the rider or driver has first to decide whether he is doing this because he is afraid or because he is full of high spirits. If he is afraid he must be taken up to the object of his terror and allowed to stretch out his nose and sniff it. He can be made to stand alongside it for a while until he has relaxed. He should not be punished neither should he be patted. If he is patted on every occasion that he shies, he may get the idea that his rider is pleased that he has swerved across the road.

Shying which is carried out through *joie de vivre* is probably best ignored.

If a horse shies out of habit he should be ridden or driven firmly past the object. Even if the habit is deliberate on the part of the horse, it is probably best not to punish him because this always seems to make matters worse.

Fear of Pigs, Donkeys, Goats etc.

There are lots of horses who are terrified of such animals as pigs, donkeys and goats. The sight or smell of such an animal causes blind panic and the horse loses his sense of reason. His reaction, very often, is flight and this can be extremely dangerous for his rider or driver.

Cause

The fear is probably caused by lack of familiarity with whatever is frightening him. Once the horse has had a severe fright by running away from a pig, donkey or goat he will then probably associate the fright with the animal and the fear will be increased.

Prevention

The simplest method of preventing a horse from developing a shyness for these animals is to introduce him to them when he is young. It is a great help to stable a horse, or have him in a field, within the sight, sound and smell of pigs, donkeys and goats. Very often, it is the smell which causes as much, if not more, trouble than the sight.

Dealing with the problem

If the horse is very frightened it is probably a good idea to borrow a donkey, pig or goat from someone who is prepared to lend one and keep it in an adjoining stable or field where it can be seen, heard and smelt. There are some horses, however, who are so afraid that they will never settle. They will become so frantic with fear that they break blood vessels in their noses, in which case this treatment is of little use. There are other horses who will accept pigs kept in an adjoining building, and even hang their heads through to rub noses, but will still be unable to face pigs if they meet them when they are being ridden or driven. If this is the case, there is little more that can be done.

Water Shy

A number of horses instinctively dislike putting their feet into water. They will perhaps shy violently across the road, towards an oncoming lorry, in preference to stepping into a shallow puddle on the path in front of them. If the animal is to be ridden or driven in events where water has to be crossed then the problem can be serious.

Cause

The fear is quite reasonable. Obviously, mountain and moorland breeds have to be careful when they run wild. Bogs, which could result in drowning, have to be avoided. It is, therefore, not surprising that horses are afraid of stepping into water, especially if it is lying on a soft bottom. Animals with Arabian blood, after all, have ancestors who began life in the desert where water is a rare sight. Therefore, as so many horses trace back to Arab or mountain and moorland breeding, it is understandable that a lot of them are afraid of crossing water.

Prevention

It is essential to build, gradually, the horse's confidence in water. He must never be asked to walk into a muddy pond where he will sink and become very frightened. It is a good idea, when riding or driving, to make a point of going through, in preference to round, every available puddle on the road. If the animal can be turned out into a field with a stream, which he has to cross to graze further, so much the better. He can have a good look and cross the water in his own time.

Dealing with the problem

If there are plans to either ride or drive the horse in events and he is really afraid of water, then a serious training scheme must be carried out.

The horse should be taken at first to a narrow and shallow ford which has a tarmac or stony bottom. It is a help to take a schoolmaster along as well, so that the nervous horse can be ridden behind and follow his companion's good example. If no older horse is available then it is up to the rider to fill his horse with confidence. If the animal is terrified, it may be a help, initially, to lead him across. Very often, a horse will be reassured when he sees his handler step into the water and will be prepared to follow. Once the horse has walked into the water he should be held there and given a titbit. Then he can be led backwards and forwards across the water several times until he becomes rather bored with the whole procedure. If he cannot be led, or ridden, into the water he may be prepared to go in if he is driven on long reins. He can be held straight with the hands and sent forward with the lunge whip from behind. If driving events are to be his job, then once he has faced water either under saddle or on long reins, he can be put to his vehicle and driven across.

It is worth taking the time and trouble to visit several

different water crossings before the horse is asked to cross water whilst under the stress of a competition. The horse may have to be boxed and travelled considerably in order to complete the training programme. It may be found that whilst the horse is quite likely to go across a stream with which he is familiar, he will be afraid of one which is strange to him.

Traffic Shy

Horses who are frightened of traffic are not safe to ride or drive on modern roads. Twentieth-century car drivers are generally unaware of the danger which they can create by driving too fast past, or too close to, a nervous horse. They are often ignorant of the speed at which a horse can react if he is frightened and do not allow for this when they meet a horse being ridden, driven or led along a road. The result of the motorist's carelessness can be a fatal accident to the rider, driver, horse or even the motorist himself.

It is essential that whoever is in charge of a horse on the road, should thank all car drivers who slow down. Failure to observe this common courtesy does tremendous harm to the relationship between horsemen and car drivers who are not horsemen. Such a driver is quite likely not to bother to slow down for the next horse which he meets and that handler will be the one to suffer for a previous person's bad manners.

Cause

Some horses are naturally frightened of traffic.

Generally, it is horses whose early life was spent in a

secluded field, who are most afraid when they have to face heavy traffic for the first time as four-year-olds either under saddle or in harness. It is a grave error to keep a youngster tucked away in a quiet park for the first four years of his life.

A severe fright can cause a horse to be bad in traffic because horses never forget such an incident.

Prevention

It is a good idea to introduce a foal to the sights and sounds of traffic as soon as possible. Ideally, the mare and foal should spend their first summer in a field which is next to a main road where there is a constant stream of heavy traffic thundering past. The foal will soon ignore the traffic and when the time comes for him to be ridden or driven, he will be traffic-proof. Of course, if the mare were very frightened of traffic she would influence the foal and make him afraid too. If this were the case, it might be better to wait until the foal is weaned and then put him into a roadside field with an old quiet pony rather than risk a bad influence from the mare.

Dealing with the problem

When ridden, he should be taken out alongside an animal who is reliable and quiet. The nervous horse can be tucked in on the nearside of the schoolmaster, whether he is being ridden or driven. This will almost certainly have a steadying effect and daily work of this kind will give the nervous horse confidence. Gradually, he will be prepared to face traffic on his own.

It is a good idea to put on some aromatic before working such a horse. Then, the horse will not smell the adrenalin which may rush through the trainer's body when, say, a double-decker bus comes round the corner. The trainer will be more confident knowing that the horse does not know that he is feeling apprehensive.

It is essential, when something large appears, not to clutch tightly onto the horse's mouth. This will cause fear in the horse and will quite likely make him afraid when he would otherwise not have been. It is best to ride or drive with the horse on the bit so that if a frightening vehicle does appear there will already be light contact on the horse's mouth and he can be kept straight without him feeling that he has been especially 'picked up' because of the approaching vehicle. It is usually a mistake to pull into a gateway to get off the road as this also demoralizes the horse and makes him apprehensive. Ideally, he should be encouraged to face the traffic and the rider or driver must sit alert, ready to react, without letting the horse know that he is expecting trouble. It is best, in fact, to try just to be prepared for trouble rather than to expect it. Horses have an uncanny way, sometimes, of sensing their handler's feelings. So to expect trouble might even lead to creating it.

Very often, a horse which is frightened of meeting a solitary vehicle along a country lane, will face any amount of traffic in a town. For this reason, it is sometimes preferable to take a horse into town traffic where, although there is a lot, it will be moving relatively slowly.

Before embarking on such schooling it is prudent to check that the third-party insurance cover is fully in order.

Refusing to Canter on a Given Leg

Some horses favour cantering on a particular leading leg and will go to great lengths to avoid cantering with the opposite leg leading.

The canter is a three-time pace. In going to the right, on the correct (inner) lead, the footfalls are: (1) near hind; (2) off hind and near fore together; (3) off fore. It may be confusing that the so-called leading leg is the last to touch the ground but in fact the pace starts from behind. It is called the leading leg because if the rider glances down it appears to be the leg which reaches forward the furthest.

If the horse is watched from the ground, when he canters on a right-hand circle, with the off fore leading, it will be seen that both off-side legs appear to sweep foward more than the near-side ones. The reverse, of course, applies to a horse cantering on a left-handed circle with the near fore leading. If, however, the horse insists on cantering with the near-side legs leading when he is going to the right he will look very ungainly. Naturally this does not apply to horses who are trained to perform counter-canter at a high level of dressage, when, in fact, they are asked to canter with the outer legs leading.

A novice horse who canters on what is known as the 'wrong leg' will look unbalanced and will be likely to cross his legs, hit his joints, and may even fall. It is therefore essential that the horse should be trained to be obedient to his rider's demands to canter with the inner legs leading. This applies particularly to occasions when the horse is competing in jumping competitions. It is much easier for the horse if he will land on whichever leg is necessary in order to turn quickly to approach the next jump which may be set in a different direction. If he solidly continues on the same leg, regardless of the direction of the turn, it is likely that valuable seconds will be lost due to his unbalanced progress. This could also result in a fence being hit owing to an incorrect approach.

Cause

The problem can relate to when the horse was handled

as a foal. If he was always led from the near-side it is quite likely that difficulties were encountered when he was broken. He was probably reluctant to go off on a right-handed circle, owing to the fact that he was not happy to allow his handler to stand on the off-side. If his trainer was lazy, he may have given in to the resistance and worked the horse only on a left-handed circle. Naturally, the horse would then always prefer to canter with the near-side legs leading.

Prevention

It is essential to work the horse, at all stages of training, equally in both directions on a circle. If he has a bad side then obviously he must be given more work on that rein than on his good side.

Dealing with the problem

The horse should be taken back to basic work on a circle, on the lungeing rein, in a cavesson. An enclosed arena, which is at least 60 feet (18 metres) across, is necessary. The horse should be made to walk, trot and halt to left and right. Canter work should be avoided at this stage. When the horse is going calmly, and is obedient to the voice he can be asked to trot over a pole on the ground. When he is happy about this, a cavalletti (see Fig. 16) can be put across the track. The horse should be worked on his bad side first, at this stage. He should be sent forward at a free-moving trot towards the cavalletti and as he takes off, he must be driven forward with the voice and whip into canter. He will almost certainly land on his inner fore leg and must be made to continue forward at the canter on this lead. As he comes round, towards the cavalletti, he should be held to the inside so that he can continue to canter. It is best not to let him canter over the cavalletti as his stride may be wrong and if he jumps awkwardly he may frighten him-

Fig. 16 Cavalletti.

self. He can be brought back vocally to trot and again sent on over the cavalletti into canter. The approach to the cavalletti is best if it is always at the trot in order to get him to go calmly and land on the desired lead into canter.

The work can then be repeated under saddle. In order to get the horse to land on the off fore, it is best, when in mid-air, to increase the contact on the right rein and for the rider to put the weight of his body a little to the right at the same time as he presses with his left leg behind the girth.

Similar work can then be carried out in a larger schooling area.

Next, the horse can be asked to go into canter without the aid of a jump. It is best to ask for the transition at the corner of an arena. The horse must be held well together between hand and leg at a balanced trot. His rider should then sit down firmly into the saddle and feel the right rein. He should push with the left leg behind the girth and right leg on the girth to get the horse off onto the off fore lead. It is sometimes a help to carry a long cutting whip which will reach the horse, behind the girth, on the left side, whilst the rider still maintains contact with the left hand on the rein. This will back up the leg aid behind the girth, and should help to get the horse off onto the right leg. Once the horse has fully understood what is required, he will probably go off into canter equally well on either leg with a delicate and unobtrusive aid. He must always be patted and praised when he obeys his rider's commands.

It is often a help to ride a continual figure of eight with a change of leg through about four strides of trot in the centre. He will soon learn to go off on alternate leads and become equally happy to lead on either leg.

On no account should the horse be asked to change legs at the centre of the figure of eight with a flying change, at this stage of training. He is likely to become unbalanced and change just his front legs. He will then continue in a disunited canter with one lead in front and a different one behind. The footfalls could be: (1) near hind; (2) off hind and off fore; (3) near fore. This is very ugly and ungainly. It is a pace which must not be tolerated.

Refusing and Rushing Fences

Horses who either rush towards their fences when they are being jumped, or who cannot be relied on not to refuse are unpleasant to ride out hunting or in competitive events.

Those who rush are likely to put up their heads so that they do not look where they are going. They then jump with a hollow back and dangling legs. This can result in them hitting the fence hard and perhaps falling.

Horses who are known to refuse are unreliable. Riding towards a fence on a horse which may, at the last minute, stop dead is not much fun. The rider has to be prepared for the horse to refuse suddenly and duck his head, and so has to be in a position which ensures that he does not get pitched over the animal's shoulder. At the same time, he must drive the horse on in an effort to prevent a refusal.

Cause

Probably the most common cause of refusing and rushing fences is fear, which results in lack of confidence.

It is quite possible to ride a horse which will never refuse a reasonable fence, because he has such trust in the person who is on his back that when he is asked to jump an obstacle, whatever it might be, he will believe in his rider.

If he is over-faced, that is asked to jump too large a fence before he has developed the necessary muscles and learnt how to fold up his legs, bend his back and lift himself and his rider over a jump, he will almost certainly become frightened and refuse. Quite naturally he will then either refuse to jump anything which appears to be large or uninviting or he will try to take charge of his rider by putting up his head and rushing towards the fence.

Sometimes a horse will frighten himself by jumping a big fence successfully but landing awkwardly. Although he may have appeared to jump satisfactorily he has perhaps given himself a fright which he will remember because the fence was too large for his capabilities or the ground was too hard or rutty.

He may hit himself on a fence which will frighten him and cause him to dislike that particular type of jump. Obviously, if he has knocked himself hard on a red wall, he may regard all red walls with a certain amount of suspicion until he regains his confidence.

Bad riding can cause a horse to refuse or rush.

If a rider gets left behind over a fence the horse may receive a jab in the mouth and a thump on his back when he lands. This will make him wary of jumping. In extreme cases, he may even get pulled down into the fence. Naturally, once this has happened, he will lose confidence in his rider and so will be very likely to refuse.

If the rider is nervous, then the smell of adrenalin which is given off by the rider will be sensed by the horse and cause apprehension.

Some horses may refuse because they are physically incapable of jumping the fence which is being requested. They may have an unsoundness in their legs or feet which causes pain, or a weakness in their back which makes jumping difficult.

Prevention

If the preliminary training is carried out carefully, then the horse should neither rush nor refuse his fences. He will probably jump correctly and calmly.

Time and patience are needed in order to train a horse to jump.

He can be started, as a three-year-old, walking and trotting over poles on the ground whilst he is being lunged. He will learn to take the poles in his stride. He should be introduced, at first, to a single solid pole which is at least 15 feet (4.5 metres) wide. He must be made to walk and trot over it in both directions until he is fully confident and does not get excited. Then, gradually the number of poles should be increased until there are about six. The distance apart will vary according to the length of the animal's stride but a rough guide is 4 feet 6 inches (1.4 metres) for a 14 h.h. animal. Obviously, these will have to be closer together for a small pony and further apart for a long-striding horse. It is important· that the animal should be able to trot comfortably over the poles so that he does not get frightened. He will learn to co-ordinate his front and back feet. He will gain confidence and build up muscles.

Once he has established his work over the poles on

the ground, he can be introduced to a small jump. A cavalletti, or similar small solid fence, can be placed 9 feet (2.7 metres) from the last of the trotting poles so that the horse will take it in his stride from the trot. A second cavalletti can be placed about 9 feet (2.7 metres) from the first (for a 14 h.h. pony). Gradually a third and then a fourth can be put into position to form a jumping grid with a trotting approach.

Next, a distance of about 18 feet (5.5 metres) can be left between the first cavalletti and the second. The third and fourth cavalletti must be moved and can gradually be used to build up the second fence. The pony must be made to jump the first cavalletti from a trotting approach and sent on into one canter stride before going over the second fence. Gradually, the second jump can be made wider and then higher. It should always be a spread fence and always have a ground line (pole on the ground in front of the fence). By being brought into the second fence with one canter stride, from the first cavalletti, he will always meet it correctly. He will gain confidence and begin to see his stride into a fence.

Once he has learnt to jump these fences without a weight on his back, he can repeat all the work with a rider.

It is essential that the training should not be hurried. On no account should the trainer be tempted to see how high a horse can jump. It is a grave error to over-jump a young or novice horse. As in all aspects of training horses, it is absolutely essential to conclude each training session on a good note so that the animal is not frightened in any way.

Dealing with the problem

Horses who have already got into the habit of refusing and rushing will benefit from the training just described in order that their confidence can be re-built.

When they are being schooled at home it is quite a good idea to place a cavalletti in front of each jump at a distance which will give one canter stride from a trotting approach so that the horse will be put exactly right for the larger fence. The horse should be circled at the trot until he is calm and then brought in over the cavalletti. He will always meet his second fence correctly and confidence will be gained. He may then settle and learn to jump off his hocks and cease to rush or refuse.

A series of fences at about 10 or 11 feet (3 metres) apart will teach him to bend his back and tuck up his front feet. This exercise will probably be of help to horses who are inclined to trail their legs or rush.

Pulling Away from the Pole

This problem sometimes occurs with pairs of horses or ponies which are driven in harness on either side of a pole, usually to a four-wheeled vehicle.

Either one, or both, of the animals leans outwards, away from the pole, with the outer side of its body pressing against the outside trace. The pole strap is pulled tightly, from the pole head, causing the collar to be pulled sideways. This can result in the outer hame tug chafing the outer shoulder. It may rub to such an extent that a sore area develops under the tug. The coupling rein will also be pulled tightly causing the horse's head to turn inwards. As the horse leans outwards, the side of his belly can also be rubbed by the outside trace.

Very often, if one horse begins to pull away from the pole, his partner will counteract the weight by pulling in the opposite direction.

In extreme cases, both of the animal's legs and feet will be found to lie at an unbelievably acute angle to the ground.

Such a pair is very unsafe to drive. There is grave danger of them slipping. Contact through the reins to their mouths is unpleasant owing to their crooked necks and inwardly turned heads.

Cause

A variety of reasons can cause a horse to pull away from the pole. Sometimes the habit develops initially when the pair are driven too fast and, in an effort to keep their balance, they lean outwards on the pole straps and outside traces. Equally, if they are tired, they may seek support from these parts of their harness and lean against them.

If a pair are put to a vehicle with their pole straps fastened too tightly they may feel restricted and lean away as a resistance. Once the habit has begun, it may continue even if the pole straps are loosened.

If a pair is always driven on the same side of the pole they may develop the habit.

Prevention

It is best continually to change the position of two horses which are frequently driven as a pair so that they will go equally well on both sides. Ideally, if two animals are driven regularly it is best to alternate pair work with single and/or tandem so that they do not go out as a pair every time that they are driven. Then, if when they are driven as a pair, they are changed from one side to another it is unlikely, if they are not over-driven, that they will ever develop this disagreeable habit.

Of course, extreme care must always be taken to see that the pole straps, coupling reins and traces are adjusted to the correct length so that the pair are comfortable in their harness.

Dealing with the problem

Once a pair has developed seriously the habit of pulling away from the pole, there is not much that can be done to stop the resistance.

It is no good tightening the pole straps or coupling reins in an effort to hold the horses together as this will almost certainly make matters worse.

Probably the only possible solution is to drive the horses in single harness for a few weeks to prevent the habit from establishing itself. Work in tandem harness can also be of use. Then, it sometimes helps to put one of the offenders in the lead of team alongside a straight going mature leader. Here, the problem horse will be working as a pair but will not have a pole to pull against and so will be more likely to keep straight. After a considerable amount of work, the offender can be put alongside a pole and he may be found to remain straight. It is, however, best to keep moving him around into varying positions of single, tandem and team so that the habit does not recur.

Leaning Against the Pole

Some horses which are driven regularly in pair harness, develop the disagreeable habit of leaning against the pole. This makes it very difficult to keep the pair straight because the partner of the offending horse is pushed continually to one side. Sometimes, as a defence, the horse who was originally innocent of the habit will push back. The result is that both animals lean at an acute angle against each other. If this happens, they will probably sweat and become sore with the friction against the pole. It is possible, if this habit is practised by the leader of a team, where there is no pole, for one leader to lean so hard against his partner that he pushes him off his feet.

Cause

Most of that already written in the previous section about pulling away from the pole applies to leaning against the pole. It can also be caused by a young and uncertain horse leaning against a mature animal when he is seeking comfort and reassurance.

Prevention

The horse must be moved from one position to another as often as possible if there is any suspicion that he is beginning to consider leaning towards the pole. Again, all that has been written in the previous section applies to this problem.

Dealing with the problem

Some people advocate the use of such artificial aids as hedgehog skins or dandy brushes fixed alongside the pole to prick the sides of a horse who tries to lean on the pole. The author has never resorted to such treatment preferring to prevent the habit, or deal with it by instantly moving the horse into a different position or putting him to alternative work such as that of single or tandem.

Keeping a Driving Bridle on a Hairy Pony

Sometimes difficulty is experienced in keeping a blinkered driving bridle on a mountain or moorland type of pony. There is grave danger of it being rubbed off against the shafts or pole. The result of such an eventuality could be a serious or even fatal accident.

Cause

The combination of a profusion of mane and forelock with small ears, causes the bridle to lie loosely at the top of the poll, with little to hold it in place. It is not feasible to tighten the throatlash enough to prevent the bridle from being rubbed off. One which is buckled very tightly will almost surely be uncomfortable for the pony. It will stop him from flexing and holding his head correctly.

Prevention

The situation would be simplified if fashion permitted about one inch of the mane to be cut away at the poll area of such breeds as Shetlands. Unfortunately, if the animal is to be shown in hand, in mountain and moorland classes, some judges and breeders feel strongly that none of the mane should be removed at the top of the neck.

Dealing with the problem

If the pony is not going to be shown in hand then the simple solution is to cut the mane to enable the head-piece to lie between the mane and the forelock.

One way of securing the bridle on a hairy pony without cutting part of the mane, is to take a strand of the forelock and pass it back over the top of the head-piece of the bridle. It is then braided into two small strands of mane just behind the head-piece to make a narrow and discreet plait. The end is then turned up and sewn with matching mane-plaiting thread. For everyday work, an elastic band is convenient. The main disadvantage of this idea is that the plait has to be undone before the bridle can be removed after work. This, however, is far outweighed by the advantage of preventing the great danger of a bridle coming off a pony whilst it is being driven.

An alternative method is to have a second throatlash point strap, and strap and buckle, sewn onto the cheek-pieces of the bridle at the base of the blinkers. This can be buckled quite tightly below the cheek bones to keep the bridle in place without putting pressure onto the throat (see Fig. 17).

Another effective second throatlash can be put onto the bridle without it having to be a permanent fixture. For this, a special browband is needed which has an extra loop on each side. A strap with a buckle and keeper at one end and a point with holes at the other is passed over the top of the head, behind the bridle head-piece, through the loops at the ends of the browband. It is secured to the back of the noseband by a small double loop of leather. One loop is threaded over the noseband buckle so that it can be taken off the noseband if it is not needed. The other loop holds the extra throatlash in place. The throatlash can be buckled quite tightly to keep the bridle in place (see Fig. 18).

This fitting is quite acceptable in the show ring for the wheeler of a tandem, whose bridle is frequently under considerable strain from the leader's reins. If the

Fig. 17 Bridle with second throatlash.

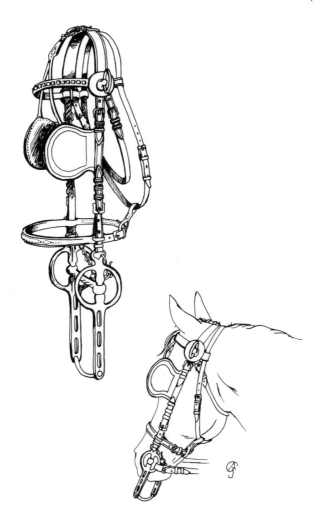

Fig. 18 Bridle with auxiliary throatlash.

leader swings round suddenly, the outer side of the
wheeler's bridle gets pulled violently by the leader's rein
passing through the wheeler's bridle terret. This can drag
the bridle off if precautions are not taken.

Banging the Door and Kicking the Wall

Horses who bang their stable doors with a front foot, or kick the wall with a hind foot, are a bore. They are likely to damage the wood and paint of the stable and injure themselves in the process. They are a nuisance at home and an embarrassment to take away on visits to friends or shows. Capped hocks and big knees can develop if the horse persistently bangs the wall or door.

Cause

Door banging is usually caused by impatient horses demanding attention or food. Some horses start banging their door as soon as the dawn breaks, in anticipation of their breakfast. Others just make a nuisance of themselves when someone is around, in order to gain attention. A shout, or even a hit with a command to keep quiet, is far preferable to such a horse than being ignored.

Some horses will stand and kick with both hind legs out of sheer frustration when a stable companion is taken out for exercise and they are left behind.

Prevention and dealing with the problem

Sometimes shutting the top door will prevent the horse from banging the lower door as he usually prefers to hang his head over in order to get his foot closer to the door. Therefore, if he is known to bang at feed times, or first thing in the morning, it is best to keep the top door shut all night and when feeds are being mixed.

A bar which is put up at the same height as the top of the lower door, about a foot inside the door, is a help. This prevents the horse from getting close to the door and his foot then does not contact the door as he scrapes the floor.

An iron grating in place of the top door may also prove effective.

If the horse bangs at other times, purely to gain attention, it is probably wisest to walk away and ignore him. This is not always easy when paint, wood and horse are all likely to be damaged, but very often such an animal will desist when he no longer has an audience.

A horse who kicks because his stable companion is taken away is best stabled in isolation with a radio for company.

There are various ways of trying to stop persistent door banging.

The hobbles which are described in a previous section and illustrated in Fig. 2 (page 23) may be effective. Although these can be left on all day when there is someone about to keep an eye on the horse, it is not safe to leave them on at night. If the horse lies down he is likely to have difficulty in getting up and may hurt himself.

Another method is to fasten separated hobbles around

the front pasterns of a door banger and hind pasterns of a kicker. About 1 foot (300 mm) of 1½-inch (35-mm) link chain is shackled to each hobble. When the horse kicks, or bangs, the chain comes back and punishes the horse, which may stop the habit. There is a danger of the horse getting more damaged by the chain than he would by the door or wall so if this method does not stop the habit quite quickly it is best left alone.

Some people prefer to use a length of cord with a small rubber ball on the end. This will bounce off the wall or door and hit the horse in response to the kick. Cord is in some ways more dangerous than chain in that it could get round a heel and cause a severe rope burn. It could also get between the shoe and the hoof of the opposite foot and bring the horse down.

Branches of gorse around the stable are said by some to be effective.

Rubber matting or sacks filled with straw can be fixed to the walls and door to protect the horse although they will not prevent the habit. Some horses will keep themselves amused by tearing the sacking off the walls, which perhaps is preferable to the kicking, but maddening for the owner who has spent a lot of care and time in putting the padding around the stable.

Probably the answer to a severe culprit is to keep him in a stall.

Horses who are tied up in stalls can be prevented from damaging themselves by straw padding being packed in sacks around the rear pillars if the stalls are of solid construction. Banging becomes restricted to pawing the ground because there is nothing within reach at the front unless the manger is the old fashioned kind with boarding which goes to the floor.

Stalls are practical and, contrary to some people's beliefs, horses can be made very comfortable. They lie down as much as if they were stabled in a loose-box. Deep straw, which is banked up at the sides, can be extremely warm.

The width of a stall for a 14.2 h.h. pony should be a minimum of 6 feet (1.8 metres) and the depth should be 10 feet (3 metres).

Neckstraps are preferable to headcollars for tethering as these allow more freedom. Also, there is the danger of the horse becoming sore behind his ears if he wears a headcollar all the time that he is tied up in his stall. The tethering rope should pass through a ring which is about 3 feet (1 metre) from the floor and then through a log (a lump of heavy wood with a hole in it). This keeps the rope taut and prevents a loop over which the horse might get a front leg. An automatic drinker is, in many ways, preferable to a bucket, which often gets knocked over and damaged by a horse who is inclined to scrape with his front feet. Wall brackets, for buckets, can be dangerous at floor level as the horse may hurt his leg.

Horses who are kept in stalls should, ideally, be allowed out daily into a field whenever practical, so that they do not have to stand for hours staring at a wall.

Climbing over the Stable Door

Horses who climb over their stable doors are not only a nuisance but they cause considerable damage to wood, paint and structure as well as to themselves. They are an embarrassment to take on visits to shows or to stay with friends owing to the uncertainty of their behaviour. Some horses restrict their climbing to putting a front foot over the top of the lower door. Worse offenders actually climb right out over the top of the door.

Cause

The gregarious nature of the horse is usually the cause

of this tendency. A horse who is stabled alone, out of sight and hearing of other horses, rarely practises the habit. A horse mostly does this when a stable companion is taken away from an adjacent loose-box and the one who is left behind is anxious to join his friend.

Prevention and dealing with the problem

The simplest solution is to shut the top door. A more pleasant method of prevention, for the horse, is to put an iron or wire-mesh grid in the area of the top door, so that the horse can still see out but cannot get his legs over the door to jump out. The danger of a mesh grid, instead of iron bars, is that it is possible for the horse to get a strand between his hoof and his shoe. If this happens, the foot could become damaged if the shoe is torn off.

Another simple solution is to fix a bar at a height which is just below halfway between the top of the lower door and the top of the top door frame. A piece of 2-inch (50-mm) galvanized steel tubing is ideal for this purpose. It can be fitted into small frames of wood on each side of the door post. The top of one of the frames can be formed by a long bolt which can be pulled out to release the bar when the horse is taken from the stable. The method is ideal for the loose-box at home but, of course, is no help when the horse is taken away to shows or to visit friends. Usually, though, once a horse has found that he cannot climb over his door, he ceases to try.

An effective method of dealing with this disagreeable habit is to put a pair of hobbles onto the horse whilst he is in the stable during the day. It is essential to take these off at night, of course, when the top door can then be shut, for reasons given in the previous section.

The author does not advise the use of hobbles on horses with a highly strung temperament owing to the danger of them hurting themselves.

Barging from the Stable

Some horses have the irritating habit of trying to push their way out of the loose-box whenever anyone opens the door to go in.

The habit can be dangerous if the animal succeeds in getting out, especially if, once out, he is free to go wherever he likes.

Cause

This is entirely caused by lack of discipline and the horse's disrespect of his handler.

Prevention

The horse must be trained to stand back whenever the door is opened. It is quite a good idea to take a small stick and tap the horse on the shoulder and say 'Get back' if he tries to push past his groom when the door is opened.

It is a good idea, when constructing new stables, to have the boxes leading out into a yard which is enclosed with rails and a gate. Then, if a horse should ever manage to get out of his stable he cannot wander onto a road and perhaps cause an accident.

Dealing with the problem

If the horse is large and strong, and the handler is small and weak, it may be of help during the early stages of disciplining the animal, to devise a means of preventing him from escaping whilst he is being corrected. Once he finds that he can no longer bully his handler, and push past as soon as the door is opened, he will give up trying. A wooden, 4 x 2 inch (100 x 50 mm) bar can be fixed by a hinge at one end to the door post on the inside. There can be a sliding bolt to the door post at the opposite end. When the stable door is opened, the bar remains in position at about the height of the horse's chest. This enables the groom to enter the loose-box but effectively prevents the horse from walking out. He must be told to stand back and will soon learn to obey. He should be caressed for doing so. It is often a help to keep a headcollar on during the day, so that he can immediately be racked up for mucking out or grooming. He will learn to accept the discipline. When all the stable work in his box is completed, he can be let loose and fed.

The rail can be opened on its hinge when the horse needs to be brought out of the stable.

Some horses barge with their head against their groom's head or body, in order to push him out of the way. This can be very painful. The author has found a certain and simple cure. She wears a motor-cycle crash helmet when she is dealing with such a horse. She does not say anything to him when he barges, nor does she hit him with her hand or a stick. She merely butts him severely in his face with her crash-helmeted head. The horse is shattered by such treatment and soon ceases to use his head as a method of pushing people out of his way.

Biting

Horses who bite are unpleasant and, in some cases, dangerous to handle.

Cause

Biting can be caused by a variety of reasons.

Possibly the most serious form of biting is that which is practised by some stallions. They tend to use their teeth and front legs, rather than their hind feet, as a method of defence. When a stallion lays his ears back and jumps forward with an open mouth, he means business. If he gets hold of someone's arm when he is in this aggressive frame of mind, he is not likely to let go in a hurry and the result can be extremely serious. He may even push his victim over and pound him with his front feet.

Colts or geldings who are turned out in a field together, often spend hours biting at each other. They will even kneel down in order to reach their playmate's legs with their teeth. This kind of biting is usually just high spirits but can later develop into domination on the part of one horse who wishes to become boss, or leader of the herd.

Excessive titbits can cause horses who would otherwise be good natured, to bite. They start to nudge pockets for lumps of sugar or similar goodies and when, one day, their owner fails to produce a titbit, they bite in disappointment. In days gone by, the milk, bread and other delivery horses in London were sometimes guilty of this habit. The horses would stand with their front feet on the pavement, having pulled their cart as far as the front wheels would allow against the kerb, whilst the tradesman was delivering goods. Some kind ladies would give the horses titbits, but less generous pedestrians handed out a smack on the nose as the animal stretched out his face towards them. The horses sometimes retaliated by biting and there were complaints to the dairy or bakery. The driver was then issued with a muzzle which had to be put onto the horse whenever necessary.

Some horses bite when they are in the stable if they are nervous of the person who is looking after them. A new groom can cause a sensitive horse to bite as a resistance, if he is not quiet and tactful in his initial approach.

Horses who have had their skin pinched when they are being saddled, harnessed or rugged up may turn and bite their handler in anticipation of pain which they are expecting, as, say, when a girth is tightened.

Gentle nips are sometimes given by a horse as a form of endearment. The horse will nuzzle his handler or another horse and then, with ears pricked, will quickly take a small bite, which can be extremely painful to the object of his affection.

Prevention

No chances should be taken with stallions. They must always be handled with respect and care. It is probably safest to carry a small stick whenever a stallion is being led. He should be trained to step back when his handler goes into the stable. It is wise to tie him to the ring on the wall whilst he is being mucked out or groomed. Simple precautions can prevent biting and a serious accident.

Horses who are nervous in the stable must be treated kindly so that they do not feel the need to bite in defence.

All girthing must be carried out with care so that skin does not get pinched.

Dealing with the problem

Some horses who bite have to be punished while others react favourably to being corrected quietly.

Occasionally, a horse will fly at his handler and try to bite him over a stable door. Such a horse can sometimes be trained with one carefully timed smack. If he is severely corrected at once, as he jumps at his victim, he may be taken by surprise and decide never to bite again. Obviously such treatment must not be practised on a horse who bites because he is nervous as it will make him even more frightened.

A nervous horse must be handled with love. It is advisable to wear a thick sweater and coat as well as heavy-duty gardening gloves so that if he should bite he will not do much damage. Titbits may help to train such a horse and make him look forward to being handled so that he will grow fond of his handler and cease to bite. Hitting is unlikely to be effective. Quiet talking and caressing is much more likely to be rewarded though it may take several months before complete mutual confidence is gained. Once the trainer has managed to stop such a horse from biting he will probably remain trustworthy with that particular person but will quite likely bite a stranger who goes into the box.

When rugging up a horse who bites because the stable roller is being girthed, it is best to tighten the roller before buckling the chest strap of the rug. This prevents the danger of the horse catching his lower jaw in the front of the rug.

A horse who bites when he is being girthed can be cured by careful girthing. If he is certain that he will never be pinched again he will, after several months, gain confidence and cease to bite. He must not be hit but just pushed away as he turns his head to nip. Again, protective clothing should be worn. Bare arms and ungloved hands are not advisable.

The author has found that one cure for a horse who nuzzles and bites from affection is to grasp the horse's nose firmly and bite him on the muzzle. The horse is surprised and learns not to nip but just to nuzzle his handler.

Rug Tearing

Some horses get pleasure from biting at their rugs and tearing them into strips. The habit is expensive and must be prevented.

Cause

Possibly the habit begins when the horse is teething as a three- and four-year-old. The desire to chew any available object is perhaps first practised on the buckle straps of the rug and roller and it is not long before the whole rug gets chewed and torn.

Prevention

It is wisest not to leave clothing on young horses if this can be avoided. The habit then will never start.

Dealing with the problem

Horses who tear their rugs usually do so when they are left alone for long periods, so it is a good plan to put on a bib each time that the horse has finished his short feeds and last thing at night. The bib resembles the rear half of a muzzle and is made of leather. It is held up by means of a strap which passes over the head and is prevented from slipping sideways by small straps and buckles which fasten to the noseband dees of the head-collar. This stops the horse from chewing at the front of his rug but is not as restricting to the horse as a complete muzzle which prevents him from eating and drinking.

Fear of Injections

A number of horses are terrified by the prospect of being injected. This can result in fear at the sight of a needle which may, in fact, only be used for plaiting a mane. Some horses are so afraid of the idea of an injection that they become difficult as soon as a veterinary surgeon walks into the stable. Even the syringe type of worm doser can cause havoc.

Cause

No one can blame a horse for being frightened of having a needle put into his neck. The author is in full sympathy with her animals as she has the same sentiments on the subject.

Prevention

It is quite possible to have a horse injected regularly against tetanus and flu, without him becoming 'needle shy'. Care must be taken on every occasion when he is injected. A headcollar should be put onto the horse and he should be held by his owner who takes the headcollar rope in the same hand that holds a large bucket of delicious food. The other hand should be laid behind the horse's eye nearest to the vet, so that the horse can see forward but not backwards.

There is a very good chance that if these simple precautions are taken on each occasion that the horse is injected, he will go through his entire life without minding the injection because probably he will not even notice that it is being done. Of course, it is essential to have a vet who is an expert and the author is fortunate to have such a person to treat her ponies which are all, apart from one, easy to inject. This stallion did not come into her hands until he was three years old, and was, by then, very nervous of needles.

Dealing with the problem

If the horse is very difficult to inject it is probably best to put a breaking cavesson onto his head to control him, in preference to a headcollar or bridle He must be placed in a corner of the stable so that he cannot escape sideways or backwards. As stated before, a bucket of food to distract his attention can be a help. A blinkered hood may simplify matters as it saves having to keep one hand over the eye and leaves both hands free to hold the horse.

If is often easier to get a needle into the horse's quarters than into his neck if he is needle shy.

Bad to Groom

Some horses dislike being groomed. This makes life difficult for whoever has the misfortune to look after such an animal as they are likely to get bitten, kicked or even squashed against a wall.

Cause

Horses who are troublesome to groom have probably been made this way by careless handlers who have been rough. If a horse has been groomed with a hard dandy brush on such sensitive places as his head and belly, and been hurt in the process, he will quite understandably grow to resent a stiff brush altogether. Animals with thin skins cannot tolerate the stiff bristles of a dandy brush on any part of their body. Once they have been hurt, they will associate a grooming session with pain and will probably become increasingly difficult. Some people use a curry comb to remove mud. Whilst this practice may be tolerated by a few thick-skinned animals it must not be employed on any but the most insensitive of creatures. Even then, it is not to be recommended.

Sudden applications of cold water can cause a horse to be afraid of being washed. There are divided schools of thought regarding the liberal use of water. If it is used, it should be applied with diplomacy. Warm water, followed by cold, is the best way to introduce a horse to being bathed. It is quite understandable that if a cold hose is suddenly directed at a horse's body or legs he will jump away. He may break his headcollar and will then become frightened. It may take a long time to get him over this initial shock.

Prevention

The horse should always be treated kindly when he is being groomed so that he grows to enjoy the sensation of having his body massaged and cleaned. He must be tied up so that he cannot walk around his box. The dandy brush should be kept strictly for removing mud and sweat from areas of the body and legs on which the horse will tolerate its use. The body brush should be used, in preference, on any sensitive parts for removing mud and sweat, as well as all over the body for taking surplus grease from the coat. A cactus cloth (which looks like a kind of rough floor cloth and can be purchased from most saddler's shops) will be found to be effective for rubbing mud and sweat off the horse if he cannot tolerate a brush.

Dealing with the problem

The horse must be handled gently. It will probably be best to use a linen cloth, or the hands, to get him used to the idea of being groomed. It is safest to use a lunge rein from the headcollar through the tie ring so that it can be held and the horse played out and quietly brought back if he should try to break loose. The cloth can be wiped over the horse, starting with his neck, all over his body. It is wise to avoid any sensitive areas for the first few sessions. Long firm sweeps with a certain amount of pressure will probably build up confidence. Too gentle handling is a mistake as it will only tickle and make matters worse. On no account should the horse be strapped at this stage as this will frighten him. It is a good idea to give the horse two or three short grooming sessions, with a titbit at the end, each day. He will probably soon grow to look forward to being groomed and will enjoy the attention he gets.

Some people advocate the use of a twitch to force a difficult horse to stand still whilst he is being groomed. Although this may be effective for a single session it cannot possibly be recommended as a long-term cure. It will only make the horse dislike being groomed even more and will reduce any hope of confidence being built up between a groom and his charge.

A front leg can be strapped up to prevent a horse from kicking. The author has never employed this treatment and does not recommend such practice. If a helper is available a front leg can be held up and that method of preventing kicking is satisfactory.

Bad to Shoe

Horses who are difficult to shoe cause a very serious problem to their owners. Good farriers are hard to find and it is not fair to expect such a craftsman to risk serious injury, which may put him out of action for several months, from an animal who is determined not to be shod. The problem will recur every four weeks so it is just not worth keeping a horse who is almost impossible to shoe.

Cause

The problem is, like most others, almost certainly caused initially by fear.

If the horse was not handled adequately when he was young, before being shod, it is understandable that he may have found the experience terrifying. This could apply even more to hot shoeing. The animal, through being troublesome, may have received a few hefty blows in his ribs with the hammer, and so it is not surprising that he disliked the whole process of being shod. Next time he would be worse and could gradually become impossible to shoe.

A horse with an injury to his back, or one of his legs, could be difficult owing to the pain suffered by having to stand on three legs, or at an awkward angle, for as long as it takes to put a shoe onto one foot.

Prevention

It is essential to pick up a young horse's feet from a very early age. If the foal has his feet picked up each day and gets used to them being cleaned out and tapped with a hoof pick, he is less likely to be frightened when the farrier comes to trim his feet. His feet should be trimmed at regular intervals until he is finally shod as a three-year-old. He will probably then accept the operation as a matter of course and will go through life without a problem.

Dealing with the problem

The horse must have his feet picked up at least twice a day when he is groomed. To begin with, it may only be possible to pick up his front feet. A great fuss must be made of him and he should be caressed, not hit. He must be made to look forward to the sessions of having his feet cleaned out and tapped gently. Slowly, he will tolerate having his feet hit quite hard with the hoof pick but it may take a very long time. Confidence has to be increased gradually until he is not afraid. When the time comes for the horse to be shod, it is essential that a quiet and experienced farrier is persuaded to do the work. A nervous man will probably, because he is afraid, hit the horse and undo all the months of quiet training in a few moments. An inexperienced farrier who takes a very long time to drive in each nail and who is so afraid of pricking the horse that he takes the nails out only to put them back in again, is equally bad.

Horses who persist in being almost impossible to shoe can be put into stocks where they are powerless to resist. The problem with this is that very few stocks are in existence.

A method which is known as 'putting the horse into shackles' is practised at some race-training stables where numerous difficult thoroughbred youngsters have to be shod for racing. Four rings are fixed into concrete on the floor in a position which enables the horse to be secured firmly as he stands on 'the pad'. Heavily padded hobble-type boots are placed around each pastern and fetlock. The horse is then secured to the ground by three legs whilst the farrier puts a shoe onto the fourth foot. The author has never seen this method but imagines that the consequences of a horse struggling violently and falling onto the floor could be tragic. Some constructions of this nature, however, have a leather-covered padded mattress to protect the horse if he should fall, but there must still be danger of injury to the horse's legs.

It is possible to give a horse a tranquillizer which enables the farrier to shoe the animal whilst it is on the ground. Obviously such treatment could not be repeated regularly.

An amusing story is told by the farrier who has shod the author's ponies for years with skill and without drama. He devised a unique method to restrain a strong-willed Shetland pony. This diminutive animal used to stand on his hind legs whenever any attempt was made to shoe him in front. The solution was simple. He was tied by his headcollar and a strong rope to the bottom of a tree, which successfully held him down. The front shoes were put on in a matter of minutes. The quiet confidence of this craftsman made the pony realize that he had met his match.

Another farrier was not so successful when he tried to deal with a donkey of similar intentions. He secured the reluctant animal to his anvil. Undeterred, the donkey merely lifted the weight and deposited it onto the poor man's foot.

Difficult to Clip

A horse who is difficult to clip creates a serious problem for an owner who intends to hunt. It is essential to clip the winter coat off a hunter at least twice, if not three times, during the season. It is usual to give the horse his first clip in October. The coat will then have time to grow sufficiently to get a tidy second clip in order to have the horse looking smart for the opening meet in November. The third clip will probably be done in time for the Boxing Day meet. It is not advisable to clip after the beginning of January because, by then, the summer coat will be starting to come through. Clipping at that time will snip the ends off the new coat. This adversely affects the shine which would later appear on the horse's summer coat. If he is going to be shown, this could be an important matter. It is less important not to clip late, with a horse who is not going to be shown that summer. Providing that the hunter is kept adequately rugged, it is usually only necessary to run the clippers lightly over the 'cat's hairs' which will appear on the lower sides of the jaw, neck, belly and at the rear of the hindquarters in January and February.

Light-grey hunters very often need clipping more frequently than dark-coloured horses who do not stain as easily.

It will be realized from the above how important it is when buying a hunter to ensure that he is good to clip. One which is not may be being sold for that very reason and is best avoided however perfect he appears to be in every other way.

Cause and prevention

The horse has probably either been roughly treated, when he has been clipped, or he may have received an electric shock. Blunt blades can cause pain if the coat gets dragged and the skin pulled. Careless clipping around such areas as the girth and stifle can cause the horse to be cut. Once the loose skin has been nipped, the horse will naturally be afraid and become difficult to clip. It is essential that the clippers should be electrically sound. Horses are very susceptible to electric shock. Once this has happened, if he has lived through the experience, he will understandably become almost impossible to clip and will probably go frantic at the mere sound of a clipping machine.

It is important to ensure that the horse is carefully introduced to being clipped so that he never gets frightened.

It is best not to give him his first clip of the season until he has been sweated a few times. This will help to remove some of the excess grease and dirt which builds up as nature's way of protecting the horse for the winter. If some of the grease is removed, before clipping, the blades will cut through the thick winter coat more readily. It is best to use new or re-sharpened blades so that they will not drag at the coat. When the girth area is clipped, it is essential that the front leg should be held forward in order to stretch the loose skin around the elbow. There will then be no wrinkles to get caught between the clipper blades and the horse will not get cut. If these simple precautions are taken when the horse is first clipped, he will not mind the sight and sound of the machine and will go through life without this problem.

It is quite possible to clip a hunter, leaving his legs and saddle patch on, in about forty minutes, providing that he gives full co-operation. If he is difficult it can take hours.

Dealing with the problem

It is sometimes a help to have the frightened horse within sight and sound of confident horses whilst they are being clipped. He can then observe their attitude and maybe will gain confidence.

It can be advantageous to make a tape recording of a quiet horse being clipped. The sound can be played every day whilst the nervous horse is being groomed. To begin with, he will probably be terrified. It is, of course, essential to be kind and sympathetic. Gradually, he may associate the sound of clippers with the soothing feeling of being quietly groomed. Once his confidence has been gained it is possible that he will tolerate being clipped.

Daily use of an electric groomer may get him to accept the idea of being clipped although a horse who is really frightened is unlikely to tolerate a groomer any more than he will accept an electric clipper.

It might be worth trying to use one of the old-fashioned hand-operated machines whereby the clipper head is driven by a cable which is geared to a wheel turned by a second person. These clippers are still in existence in some saddle rooms and once oiled and re-sharpened will readily come back into service.

It is possible to remove small areas of coat with double-handled hand clippers but it would not be practical to clip the whole horse in this way.

It is a help if there is someone who will hold the horse's headcollar rope and also hold up a front leg when ticklish areas have to be clipped. The horse is less likely to kick when he is on three legs. If a leg has to be held up it is easier to hold the foot by the horse's toe. He then puts less weight onto his holder than if his foot is clasped at the widest point or his leg held near the coronet.

The use of the twitch can be effective on some horses but the writer prefers to gain the horse's confidence rather than to use such aids.

Some horses are initially terrified of having their heads and ears clipped. It is usually better to leave such areas than to resort to a twitch. Very often, as time progresses and after several clipping sessions, the horse will allow his handler to remove more and more hair as confidence is gained. Eventually, it is likely that such a horse will stand quietly whilst his head (if not his ears) is clipped all over. One of the author's horses, Ali, at one time would not tolerate the clippers anywhere near the top of his neck, let alone his head. Now, at nineteen, he lowers his face and stretches the skin around his throat and jaw to make it easy for the author to clip his whole head. The twitch has never been used.

If the horse has to be forcibly clipped then a veterinary surgeon should be consulted. He can give the animal a tranquillizer which will either subdue him or, in extreme cases, put him right out on the floor. Obviously, this kind of treatment cannot be repeated on every occasion when the horse needs clipping.

Some horses will continue to kick, strike out or bite in spite of a mild tranquillizer. They will also fight against a twitch and in fact become impossible to twitch after they have suffered the pain a few times. This usually only works on an innocent horse who has never been subjected to such treatment before. It is certainly not to be recommended as a long-term cure.

The only real answer is to persevere quietly and calmly every day in the hopes that gradually the horse will gain confidence and trust his handler with the machine.

Extreme cases who are determined not to be clipped, may 'have to be given best'.

Difficulty in Pulling a Mane or Tail

Some horses object strongly to having hair which is considered by some people to be surplus, pulled from their manes or tails. Fashion decrees that certain horses and ponies should have the hair removed from the sides of their docks in order to make the top of the tail look as narrow as possible. This is practised on such animals as show ponies, show hacks and hunters. The main reason is that when the tail is narrowed to a minimum, the quarters, from behind, appear to be larger, rounder and stronger than they would if they were partly covered in hair spreading sideways from the top of the dock.

Exhibitors of Arab and mountain and moorland breeds, however, take an enormous pride in full, unpulled tails on their charges. Many American breeders also have the same sentiments and proudly spread their horses' tails widthways, at the top, to show off their splendour, not caring that the hindquarters are partly hidden.

All that which has been said about tails can also be applied to manes. Whilst the show pony hack and hunter fraternity like to reduce their animals' manes to a minimum, in order to obtain a row of small and neat plaits, the Arab and mountain and moorland breeders take great trouble to grow manes on their animals which will reach well down their necks, to match their tails.

Cause

It is not surprising that a horse will object strongly if a groom tries to pull too much hair from a mane or tail. Severe pulling can be very painful and can cause the horse to bleed as the roots are vigorously torn in great bunches from the skin at the sides of the dock or the underneath of the mane. Once a horse has been hurt in this way, he will understandably be wary whenever anyone tries to pull his mane or tail again.

Matters will be made worse if he is punished for objecting. His dislike is, after all, created by pain and will be increased if even more discomfort has to be endured.

Prevention

It is important to treat the horse as quietly and gently as possible when hair has to be pulled from his mane or tail. Care must be taken to remove only a few hairs at a time so that the horse does not become sore. It is better, by far, to spend several days over pulling a mane or tail than to try to complete the job at one attempt.

When pulling a mane, the hair must be taken from the underside of the mane so that the upper layer is left untouched to lie neatly down from the top of the neck. Hair can be pulled out either with the fingers or with a metal mane comb. Whichever method is used it is important that the mane should be taken by the roots, and not broken, otherwise the result will not be satisfactory.

If a tail is pulled, a few hairs at a time must be taken from the very edges of the dock, for about three quarters of the way down the dock. Hair should not be removed from the upper side of the dock or the result will be untidy. Long hair, growing from the top of the dock, is easier to keep in place with bandaging than a lot of short hairs, which are inclined to sprout sideways.

Once a tail has been severely pulled it usually requires regular pulling in order to keep it tidy. If left untouched for about a year it will probably grow sufficiently for it to be plaited. So, unless there are plans for constant maintenance it is best to leave the hair on the dock well alone and rely on plaiting for the occasions when smartness is required.

Dealing with the problem

If the horse refuses to allow his groom to pull his tail in the normal way, it may be better to leave the tail unpulled rather than resort to complicated methods.

If, however, the owner is determined for some reason that the tail must be pulled, then effective tactics will have to be devised.

Obviously it is not safe to stand directly behind such a horse as there is grave danger of getting kicked.

One method is to back the horse up to a stable door of a suitable height. He is then held in position by an assistant and given food to divert his attention. A second person could hold up one front foot to help to prevent kicking. Some people put a hobble around a hind leg and hold that forward in preference to picking up a front leg. A rope halter can be effective for this practice but care has to be taken that a rope burn is not created in the hind heel if the horse struggles. The groom then reaches over the door to remove a few hairs from the dock, each day, until the job is completed. If the animal should kick violently, he will only hit the door.

It is wise to put hock pads onto the horse to lessen

the chance of damage to his hocks if he should hit the door. It is also a good idea to bandage his hind legs for the same reason.

Clippers or trimming scissors are used by some people on the hair at the sides of the dock. Although this method may be a quick and simple way of tidying the tail, the result is fairly disastrous once the hair grows. It sprouts sideways, resembling an outgrown crew-cut, and takes well over a year to recover.

Horses who object to having their manes pulled may have the hair thinned from the underside with mane thinning scissors.

Hogging is another solution although this is not particularly fashionable now, other than for show cobs or driving animals.

As with similar problems, a number of people just resort to the use of a twitch on the upper lip in order to force the horse to stand still. Some people put a twitch onto the horse's ear. This should never be done.

Growing a Hogged Mane

There is a general misconception that once a horse's mane has been hogged it can never be grown and laid satisfactorily. It is thought by many people that it will always look thick and unruly. It is true, however, that if the mane is not trained, whilst it is growing, the end product may not be as pleasing. It is also true that it takes about nine months before the mane will lie naturally and remain on the off-side of the neck even when the animal is left ungroomed in the field.

Cause, prevention and dealing with the problem

If the growing hogged mane is left unattended it will probably assume a central parting and hang on each side of the neck. It will become thick and unruly and be difficult to plait neatly. It will look extremely untidy when it is not plaited.

After about six months of growth, when the mane is just beginning to fall to one side, it should be plaited onto the off-side in twelve or more plaits. The ends should be sewn with mane-plaiting thread, or darning wool, and left hanging down. These plaits must remain for about a week before being taken out. The mane will then be found to lie on the off-side.

Once the mane is lying properly on the off-side of the horse's neck, some of the underneath hairs should be pulled out daily until the mane is reduced to the desired thickness. It will be found that the mane can be further trained to lie on the off-side if an elastic hood, known as a 'mudguard', is used. These can be obtained from J. Cross, Cobbacombe Farm, Huntsham, Tiverton, Devon.

The mane must be water brushed or laid with hair spray and carefully pushed into position under the hood. It will be found, after about six weeks, that the mane will lie firmly and neatly in place. No one would ever know that it had been hogged.

Mane-Plaiting Difficulties

Very often difficulties are experienced when plaiting a mane because the horse, who may be young or nervous, will not keep still. Apart from being unable to plait up successfully there is also a danger of losing the plaiting needle in the bedding.

Cause

Constant head shaking can result in the plaiting needle being thrown from the plaiting thread. The needle then falls onto the bedding and it is usually impossible to find.

The author once lost a needle at three o'clock in the morning when she was preparing a pony for a show about 120 miles away. A large and vicious mosquito had been buzzing around noisily whilst the pony, a four-year-old, was being plaited. It caused the pony to give one violent shake as the forelock plait was being sewn into place. The thread was short and the needle fell onto the straw bedding. The pony was quickly taken to a different stable so that the straw remained unmoved. Close inspection, with a torch to give extra light, failed to recover the needle. The whole of the bed, which had been laid in preparation for a late return, had to be cleared out and carted to the muck heap. Even then, there was a fear that the needle might be lurking some-where to find its way into a horse at a later date. Fortu-nately, it is now nearly four years since the incident and there have not been any mysterious lamenesses amongst the author's animals. By now, surely, the needle must have rusted away?

There was a well-known show animal who suffered from intermittent lameness which was apparently inexplicable. Finally, the creature was put down. A needle was found in its shoulder.

Prevention and dealing with the problem

If a mane is to be plaited for occasions such as showing, hunting or racing it is essential that it should be pulled to a manageable length and thinness. Thick and long manes are difficult to put into neat plaits.

Manes were traditionally put into seven plaits, with an eighth for the forelock, for a hunter. Now, people tend to put the mane into any number of plaits.

It will be found that wool is far easier to use than mane-plaiting thread for securing the plaits. It can be bought in any colour to match the mane. A very large, almost blunt type of darning or tapestry needle is necessary. The wool is threaded through the needle and secured at one end around the eye in a simple overhand knot. Then, if the horse should shake his head when the plait is being sewn, the needle will remain secured to the wool and will not drop onto the floor.

The mane should be well combed and water-brushed to lay all the loose ends in place. It is then combed again and the hair for the first plait is divided from the rest of the mane. Usually, the width of the mane comb gives about the right amount for a plait. The comb is pushed into the mane which is not being plaited so that it is kept out of the way. The first section of mane is then plaited right down to the end of the hair and secured with the wool by the needle. The end of the plait is turned underneath a small amount and sewn into place. It is then turned under for a second and perhaps a third time, being sewn at each turn. It finally forms a neat and tight ball which is sewn securely into position. The stitches must be kept as invisible as possible. The wool is then broken off close to the plait.

Another advantage of wool over mane-plaiting thread is that it is unnecessary to use scissors to cut it as it can be broken by hand.

Unplaiting a mane which has been secured with wool is far easier than unplaiting one which has been sewn with thread. If the plait is held upwards, the wool stitches are clearly visible and as each is snipped with scissors, so the plait will unfold. Thread is more difficult to distinguish from the mane. Careless grooms can cause tremendous harm to manes by cutting the hair in mistake for thread. If this is repeated throughout a hunting or showing season the horse's mane becomes severely damaged and diminished.

If the horse is needle-shy, it is a good idea to tie him

on a short rope to a ring on the stable wall. For such a horse, the plaiting should start at the withers and work up towards the head, by which time he will understand that he is being plaited and not injected. It took one of the author's horses, Ali, nearly a year before he would tolerate his mane being plaited from the top of his neck towards his withers, which of course is the easier way. With a nervous horse it is a help to use a rusty needle in preference to one which is shiny. Rusty scissors make unplaiting a wary horse easier too.

Refusing to Drink

A horse who refuses to drink causes a serious problem for his owner. He will become dehydrated and lose condition.

Cause

Automatic drinkers can prevent a horse from drinking if he gets frightened by the sound of water refilling as the ball valve sinks.

A dirty bucket or dirty trough can deter a horse from drinking.

A water container which has a distasteful smell may be rejected.

A change of water with perhaps more fluoride than that to which he is accustomed, can stop a horse from drinking.

If a horse is nervous, he may refuse to drink. Horses, in their wild state, exposed themselves to great danger when they went down to the water hole to drink. It was here that predators would wait for their victims. Therefore, it still comes naturally to a horse to be wary when he is drinking. If he hears a noise or is disturbed while he is drinking, it is quite likely that he will not return to drink for some time. Horses must be left quietly to drink in peace.

Prevention

It is quite a good idea to take water in large plastic containers from the home source when travelling away to a show or for a brief visit to a friend. The usual water bucket should also be taken. This can encourage a poor drinker to drink when he might otherwise not have done so. It also reduces the risk of infection which may be carried through buckets and troughs in strange surroundings.

It is essential that clean water is available in the horse's stable at all times. The old-fashioned practice of not leaving water in the stable but leading the horse out to the trough to drink, two or three times a day, was very bad indeed and must never be applied.

Dealing with the problem

Sometimes the presence of a salt-lick hanging on the wall will encourage the horse to lick and become thirsty enough to drink.

If the horse is a good feeder, it will be possible to add rock salt or table salt to the feeds to make the horse thirsty.

Boiled food, such as barley, is a good way of putting fluid into a horse who will eat but not drink. Barley absorbs a tremendous amount of water when it is left in the oven to cook slowly overnight.

Chaff which is put into a sack and soaked overnight in a tub of clean water, is another method which can be effective in getting water into a reluctant drinker. There is no reason why the hay ration should not be fed entirely as soaked chaff providing that the horse is introduced to this carefully, in small quantities to begin with, so that he does not get colic. This is also useful for horses with coughs.

Sugar-beet pulp, which contains a lot of water after it has been soaked for twenty-four hours, is another idea.

Great care must be taken to clean the manger after every feed if wet food is given, because it quickly goes sour.

If the drinking problem persists, it is best to seek veterinary advice.

Refusing to Eat

Horses who refuse to eat cause considerable worry for their owners. It is not long before they lose condition and become an embarrassment to their rider or driver. It is very difficult to produce such a horse for exhibition in the show ring.

Cause

The problem can be caused by a multitude of reasons.

A horse who is worried is likely to go off his food. He can be disturbed mentally by a change of environment. If he is suddenly put into a different stable he may be affected by unusual smells, sounds and sights which will prevent him from relaxing enough to enjoy his food.

If he has, in the past, been hunted, the sound of hounds within the vicinity of his stable may make him so excited that he will not eat.

A horse, on return from hunting, may have become so over-excited, or over-tired, by the sport that he will refuse to eat for several days.

Sometimes, horses who are regularly hunted will not touch their food on the morning before going hunting because of the anticipation of all the fun. The same can apply to horses who are shown or jumped publicly.

Horses who are being prepared for racing tend to go off their food if the trainer tries to increase the corn ration to more than the horse can absorb.

A dirty manger which has stale remains in the corners can put a horse off his food.

Some horses dislike a change of food and will happily consume one batch of corn but refuse the next. There is, in such a case, the possibility that the grain has been contaminated by mice or cats if it has been stored where such livestock have been running over and fouling it.

Hay is frequently rejected because it is of inferior quality. Mould or dust caused by inefficient hay-making can result in extremely unpalatable food.

If the horse goes off his food for no apparent reason, there is a possibility that he is unwell. If his coat is staring he may have a cold or flu or a sore throat.

Some horses get sharp edges to their molars and these can cause a sore mouth which makes chewing uncomfortable.

Prevention

Feed bins and mangers must be kept scrupulously clean,

being washed out after each feed so that no stale food lurks in the corners. The same applies to stirring utensils such as wooden spoons, and to buckets in which the food is carried.

On hunting or showing mornings it is best to try to keep to the usual routine regarding feeding and mucking out etc., so that, even though the schedule of the day may bring the feeding time forward, the order of the routine should remain unaltered until the horse has consumed his breakfast. It is often possible to get a small feed into an unsuspecting horse before he realizes that he is being taken out for the day.

Feeds should be given little and often. Any food which is left from a previous meal must be removed. New food should not be put on top of old food. Such things as sugar-beet pulp and bran quickly go sour.

When buying hay, it is best to insist on high quality. If the animal is being hunted or put to hard work, then hay which is grown specially from seed and carefully made to retain the head, nose and colour is more likely to be readily consumed. Ponies, who are unlikely ever to refuse their food, will happily eat, and do well on, meadow hay. Bad quality hay must never be fed as it can be very harmful to the animal's wind. It will not put much condition onto the horse and so is false economy.

Dealing with the problem

Very often a poor feeder can be tempted by adding slices of carrot or apple to the feed. The secret can lie with variety. If so, the horse should get something a little different at each feed throughout the day. Numerous additives are available and worth trying. Different horses like different things. Such items as black treacle, grass meal, seaweed, liquid blackcurrant, cod liver oil, peppermint, minerals and linseed, can all be tried as an addition to the oats, maize, barley, bran, nuts and sugar-beet pulp.

A horse will frequently consume a hot linseed bran mash on returning from hunting, when he would otherwise refuse to eat.

If linseed is fed, it is essential that it is properly cooked. This is simple if a four-oven Aga is available. About 4 ounces (100 grams) of linseed should be put into a 5-pint (3-litre) saucepan with about 3 pints (1.5 litres) of water. This is brought to the boil and stirred to keep it from boiling over. When linseed boils over, the stove becomes covered with small seeds which cling affectionately to every available surface, so this must be avoided. When the mixture has thickened a little, the saucepan can be put into the simmering oven where it should be left, all day, ready for the horse in the evening. It can then be poured onto half a bucket of bran. More boiling water can be added, as desired, as can boiled barley and Epsom salts.

Green meat such as lucerne can also tempt a poor feeder.

Sometimes half an hour at grass, each day, will work wonders.

Some horses enjoy milk, in which case it is worth giving them a couple of pints out of a bucket to help maintain their condition.

The addition of a tablespoonful of cider vinegar to the horse's feed can sometimes encourage a poor feeder. A racehorse who was refusing to eat and becoming painfully thin, was apparently completely won over by this treatment.

Bolting Food

Horses who bolt their food can cause concern to their owners because it is possible that they do not chew properly before they swallow. Such rations as whole oats may pass through the animal and be seen in the droppings. Consequently they will not have done any good to the horse. If he constantly bolts his food, he is likely to lose condition as his digestive system may become upset.

Cause

This habit can be caused by an owner feeding a number of horses who are turned out in a field together, and are given short feeds in bins once or twice a day in addition to their grazing. Some horses soon discover that if they eat their own feed quickly there will be more chance of stealing another horse's ration. Others will be forced to eat quickly because they know that if they do not hurry the greedy horses will chase them away before they have finished.

Horses can also be encouraged to bolt their food if they are not left quietly to eat but are disturbed by being groomed or saddled before they have finished.

Prevention

Horses should always be fed separately so that they are not worried by other horses.

It is essential that the animal should be left in peace to eat and digest his food. At least an hour should pass between the time that he is given a short feed and when he is harnessed or saddled for work.

Dealing with the problem

Quite often, the addition of a double handful of chaff to the nuts or oats will prevent a horse from bolting his food. The chaff will make the food seem less exciting and so the horse will probably not be in such a hurry to consume his feed.

If the horse still bolts his food after chaff has been added, then it is quite a good idea to put some lumps of rock salt in the manger. The food becomes mixed and hidden under the pieces of salt and the horse has to search under the lumps for his food. The addition of salt is also favourable as a conditioner.

If the horse is seen to drop food from the sides of his mouth when he eats, it is advisable to get veterinary advice because he may need the edges of his molars filed. These can become very sharp and affect the horse's mastication and therefore his condition.

It is a grave error to hand feed an animal in order to prevent him from bolting his food. The author knows of a pony who was undoubtedly made extremely bad tempered by such treatment. He both kicked and bit by the time he was two years old, and was an extremely unpleasant animal to handle in the loose-box. It is likely that the frustration which he suffered by his owner hand feeding him at every meal caused his temper to rise and resulted in him growing to dislike people intensely.

Bed Eating

Some horses insist on munching steadily through their straw bed as soon as they have finished their short feed and hay. The tendency more usually applies to ponies whose diet is being restricted in order to prevent them from becoming too fat. The habit frequently results in the pony developing a cough. It also causes ponies to put on weight which the owner is trying to keep off them by bringing them in from the field.

Cause

Horses usually eat their beds because they are greedy. Some, if they are not being given adequate food, may eat their straw because they are hungry. Horses in training, may eat their beds because their hay ration is being restricted. Others develop the habit because they are bored.

Prevention

One way of preventing a horse from eating his bed is to dilute a little mild disinfectant and spray it lightly over the straw. Of course, if the pony is an extreme bed eater, care must be taken not to make him ill if he is likely to insist on eating his straw, even if it is flavoured with disinfectant.

Dealing with the problem

The simplest way of dealing with horses who eat straw bedding is to use an alternative floor covering. Peat, flaked paper, wood shavings or sawdust make a good bed. Peat and shavings can be bought in bales and sawdust can often be collected in sacks from timber merchants.

Care must be taken to manage these beds correctly. If they are not kept properly clean it is possible for maggots to breed, in hot weather, in the bedding.

The droppings must be lifted regularly and the wet patches removed as often as possible. The bed should be swept to the sides each day and the floor allowed to dry. Areas around the water bucket and feeding containers must be cleaned daily.

A miniature wooden rake with a short handle is ideal for removing droppings from this kind of bedding as it can be used in conjunction with a skip. A garden trug is useful for this purpose as it is easier to handle than a large skip, which becomes too heavy. A garden rake is best for pulling the bed down after the floor has been dried.

Weaving

Horses who have discovered how to weave are almost incurable. The horse rocks sideways from one front foot to the other as he looks over his stable door. This habit can result in loss of condition as the horse takes a lot out of himself when he could otherwise be resting. Some horses weave so violently that they sweat with the effort. A severe weaver will rub his chest raw against the door of the stable and tear the front of his rugs as he rocks to and fro.

There is a danger of horses in boxes adjacent to the weaver, copying the habit. It is best to avoid having a weaver in one's possession.

Cause

Weaving is generally caused by boredom. Horses are frequently left for twenty-three hours, shut up in an area of twelve feet square, with nothing much to amuse them. It is not surprising that they develop stable vices to pass the time.

Prevention

It is essential to think of ways of keeping the horse occupied throughout the day.

Frequent, very small feeds are a help. A hay-net to pull at, will keep the horse amused. A salt-lick is welcome. A period at grass each day prevents boredom.

A radio which is left playing when nothing else is happening in the yard, is sometimes appreciated.

It is a help if the stable looks out into a yard, or the open, in preference to a passageway where there is nothing for the horse to watch.

Some horses like to have a toy with which to play. The author kept her stallion amused for years with a motor tyre which was cut, rolled up and secured with a bolt so that it resembled a rugger ball. This was hung by a chain from a rafter in the stable roof. The horse would canter round his box, which was about twenty feet by eighteen feet, and punch and bite his 'toy' which provided him with endless fun.

Dealing with the problem

A specially designed grating can be put up, at the door, which has a head-sized 'V' cut out of the centre. This enables the horse to look over but prevents him from rocking from side to side. Another possibility is to hang two blocks of wood from the upper door frame. If the horse tries to weave he hits his head. Determined weavers will, however, happily weave inside the door when they are prevented from hanging their heads over the top.

Crib-biting

Crib-biting is one of the most serious stable vices. Horses which are advertized as 'has been seen to crib-bite hence low price' should generally be avoided.

The vendor will probably be careful to keep the horse occupied with a hay-net when the possible purchaser is in the stable yard and is likely to assure this unwary buyer that 'he only does it when he is moved to a new stable but he will soon settle.' Unfortunately, this statement usually turns out to be optimistic.

A horse which crib-bites presses his upper central incisors down onto any available ledge such as a stable door. He then arches his neck, opens his mouth, draws in breath and gulps as he swallows. A confirmed crib-biter will stand for several minutes taking numerous gulps of air before moving away. The habit appears to be as vital to the horse's mind as smoking is to someone who is addicted to tobacco.

A crib-biter usually loses condition as the habit affects his digestive system. It can be extremely difficult trying to keep flesh on such a horse throughout the hunting season.

Even if the horse is not actually seen to crib-bite, when he is being viewed for possible purchase, the severity of the problem can be observed by the condition of his teeth. The central upper incisors of a confirmed crib-biter will be worn and chipped at the front, through constant pressure onto hard objects.

Cause

Crib-biting is another vice which is probably caused initially by boredom.

It could also be passed from a mare to her foal who may begin by copying his mother before discovering that he too gets pleasure from the disagreeable habit.

Prevention

As with weaving, it is essential to prevent the habit from starting by trying to occupy the horse's mind throughout the long and boring hours he may have to be left shut up in a stable.

It is best to keep a crib-biting horse away from other horses who may copy the habit and then become addicted. The author, however, has proved that it is possible to keep a non crib-biter alongside a crib-biter without the habit being passed on.

The horse to which the author refers has stood for four years alongside a confirmed crib-biting hunter without developing the habit. Throughout the winter, they are in adjacent loose-boxes, and during the summer they are turned away together in a field. The non crib-biting horse was fifteen years old when these two horses were first kept together and it was decided to take a chance as circumstances made it impractical to keep them apart. The author would not, however, put any of her younger animals within sight or sound of this crib-biter.

Dealing with the problem

It is almost impossible to stop a horse from crib-biting once he has the habit. It can sometimes be checked by putting wire mesh over every ledged surface in the stable. A bar put slightly inside the top door, halfway up, prevents the animal from grabbing the top of the lower door. Feeds should be given on the floor as there must not be a manger or hay rack for the horse to grasp. Water can be left in a low-edged, large trough on the ground. An iron, circular pig-feeding bowl is ideal for this purpose.

Anti-crib-biting straps sometimes act as a deterrent. There are a number of different kinds. They all fasten around the horse's neck at the gullet. The least successful consists of an inch-wide strap with a heart-shaped piece of leather sewn onto the centre. The theory is that the shaped leather should lie against the windpipe and press into the throat when the horse arches his neck to draw a gulp of wind. In fact, the shaped piece does not stay in place and the strap will be found to rotate round the neck doing no good whatsoever. Another kind has a leather-covered metal arch which is designed to fit over

Fig. 19 Anti-crib-biting strap.

the windpipe. This does not stay in place and will also be found to spend as much time at the side of the neck, where it does no good, as over the windpipe where it acts as a deterrent. The most efficient kind of anti-crib-biting strap is the sort which has a heavy hinged metal arch onto which the leather strap is riveted (see Fig. 19). When the horse arches his neck, the metal presses hard against the lower part of the windpipe and the gulp is less satisfactory to the horse. The weight of the metal fitting causes it to return to below the neck when the horse lowers his head to feed, so it does not remain on the side of the neck as do the other kinds of strap.

A method which is said to be used by some people is to give the horse a mild electric shock by running a wire along a surface such as the top of the door. The wire must be electrified by farm electric-fencing equipment and *never* from the mains, of course.

Some people advocate that lumps of charcoal in the manger will deter a horse from crib-biting as they aid digestion.

There are various preparations which can be smeared along ledges to deter the horse from putting his mouth into crib-biting positions owing to the disagreeable smell and taste. These may be effective with some horses.

Some veterinary surgeons will operate in an effort to put an end to the habit, so it is worth discussing the problem with an expert.

Wind-sucking

Horses who wind-suck will stand in their stables and draw in gulps of breath which they then swallow. It is a similar stable vice to crib-biting but the animal does not have to catch hold of an object to fulfil the action. As with crib-biters, such horses are best left with the prospective vendor.

Wind-suckers generally lose condition. They become pot-bellied and stark in their coats.

Cause

This is similar to crib-biting and weaving.

Prevention

Again, the same applies as with other stable vices.

Fig. 20 Flute bit.

Dealing with the problem

It can be a help to leave a flute bit (see Fig. 20) on the horse when he is in the stable, other than when he is feeding. As he tries to draw air through his mouth, the wind escapes through the holes in the bit.

Index